Bringing Out the Algebraic Character of Arithmetic

From Children's Ideas to Classroom Practice

STUDIES IN MATHEMATICAL THINKING AND LEARNING
Alan H. Schoenfeld, Series Editor

For more titles in this series please visit www.erlbaum.com

Bringing Out the Algebraic Character of Arithmetic

From Children's Ideas to Classroom Practice

ANALÚCIA D. SCHLIEMANN
Tufts University

DAVID W. CARRAHER
TERC

BÁRBARA M. BRIZUELA
Tufts University

LEA LAWRENCE ERLBAUM ASSOCIATES, PUBLISHERS

2007 Mahwah, New Jersey   London

Lawrence Erlbaum Associates, Inc., Publishers
10 Industrial Avenue
Mahwah, New Jersey 07430
www.erlbaum.com

Cover design by Kathryn Houghtaling Lacey

Library of Congress Cataloging-in-Publication Data

Schliemann, Analúcia Dias.
    Bringing out the algebraic character of arithmetic : from children's ideas to classroom practice / Analúcia D. Schliemann, David W. Carraher, Bárbara M. Buizuela.
        p.   cm. — (Studies in mathematical thinking and learning)
    Includes bibliographical references and index.
ISBN 0-8058-4338-8 (cloth : alk. paper)
ISBN 0-8058-5873-3 (pbk. : alk. paper)
1. Arithmetic—Study and teaching (Elementary). 2. Algebraic logic—Study an teaching (Elementary). I. Carraher, David William. II. Brizuela, Bárbara M. III. Title. IV. Series.
QA135.6.S427   2005
372.7—dc22   2005051018
                                                                       CIP

Printed in the United States of America
10   9   8   7   6   5   4   3   2   1

Contents

7 Discussion   119

Preface
Rethinking Early Mathematics Education

People generally think that arithmetic should precede algebra in the curriculum. They can find ample evidence to support their view: Arithmetic is easy; algebra is difficult. Arithmetic is about operations involving particular numbers; algebra is about generalized numbers. Arithmetic appears in all cultures; algebra appears only in some, and, even in those, it made its appearance only recently.

However, what if there were good reasons for thinking otherwise? What if there were compelling research showing that young students can learn algebra? What if there were good mathematical justifications for teaching algebra early? What if history were not always a trustworthy guide for ordering topics in the mathematics curriculum?

Recently, following proposals by researchers in mathematics education, the National Council of Teachers of Mathematics (NCTM, 1997, 2000) has endorsed an early introduction to algebra and recommended that algebraic activities start at the very first years of schooling and that algebraic notation be introduced between Grades 3 and 5.

Many people react to these ideas with puzzlement and outright skepticism. They wonder about issues of:

- Possibility: Can young students learn algebra? Can teachers teach algebra to young students?

- Desirability: Is it important or useful for students to learn algebra early (or at all)?
- Implementation: How can the recommendations for early algebra be put into effect?

This book is part of an ongoing effort to establish a research basis for the introduction of algebraic concepts and notation in elementary school, an area of studies that has come to be known as *Early Algebra*. Our research helps clarify the question of possibility, specifically, the issue of whether young students can reason algebraically. Generally, the results are encouraging—however, more than a simple yes or no answer is needed. For Early Algebra is not the Algebra I syllabus taught to young students. And algebraic reasoning is not synonymous with methods for using algebraic notation and for solving equations. As Kaput (1998) noted, algebra encompasses pattern generalization and formalization; generalized arithmetic and quantitative reasoning; syntactically guided manipulation of formalisms; the study of structures and systems abstracted from computations and relations; the study of functions, relations, and joint variation; and the modeling and phenomena-controlling languages.

In the next section, we describe our rationale for rethinking the roles of arithmetic and algebra in the mathematics curriculum and for Early Algebra. The chapters that follow provide evidence bearing directly on the issue of children's capability to reason algebraically and to learn algebra.

RETHINKING THE RELATIONSHIPS BETWEEN ARITHMETIC AND ALGEBRA

Early Algebra is not so much about *when* as *what*, *why*, and *how*. It also concerns novel views about arithmetic, algebra, and how they are related.

The prevailing view in the United States has long been that arithmetic and algebra are largely distinct subject matters standing in a particular order. As Fig. P.1 illustrates, arithmetic and algebra are traditionally conceived as largely distinct. Certain ideas, techniques, and representations are common to both; these correspond to the region of intersection (with hatched lines). Consistent with this view is the notion that arithmetic and algebra need to be

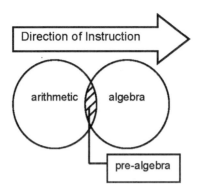

FIG. P.1.   The prevailing view of how arithmetic relates to algebra.

bridged. The bridging is seen as occurring toward the "end" of arithmetic and the "beginning" of algebra.

Pre-algebra courses offered 1 or 2 years prior to Algebra I attend to this view of arithmetic and algebra. In these courses, special attention is given to the expanded uses and meanings of symbols from arithmetic. But this *transition* is anything but simple; part of the reason for this lies in the unfortunate ways concepts have been treated in early mathematics curriculum. Consider, for example, the equals sign (=). In most arithmetic instruction, the equals sign has the sense of "yields" or "makes." Students demonstrate that they subscribe to this notion when they read the sentence "3 + 5 = 8" as "three plus five makes eight." They may even cheerfully accept expressions such as "3 + 5 = 8 + 4 = 12." But they reject "8 = 3 + 5" and "3 + 5 = 7 + 1."

When students begin algebra instruction, they are expected to treat the equals sign as a comparison operator expressing an equivalence relation. But as the previous examples testify, of the three properties of an equivalence relation—reflexivity, symmetry, and transitivity—students often do not recognize the latter two.[1]   —

This makes the difficult task of introducing algebraic equations all the more daunting. Consider, for example, an equation with variables on each side (e.g., $3x = 5x - 14$). Students have to contend with the idea that the expressions on each side of the equals sign can be viewed as a function having variation. The equals sign effectively constrains the values of

---

[1]It is not even clear whether students would accept an expression such as "3 + 1 = 3 + 1," which exemplifies the reflexive property.

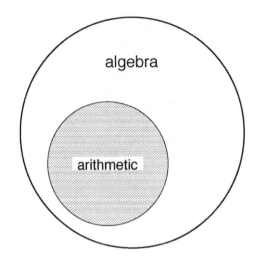

FIG. P.2.   Arithmetic as having an inherently algebraic character.

each function to the same solution set: x is free to vary, but the equation is only true under the solution set. The reader can imagine the difficulty a student will have comprehending these weighty ideas if she is still working with the understanding that the equals sign merely separates what you start with (and intend to do) from what you end up with. The situation is even more challenging when one considers the diverse roles the equals sign serves (Usiskin, 1988) in the case of formulas, identities, properties, functions, and so on.

There is an alternative to having students relearn mathematics when they take Algebra I. That alternative rests on a strikingly different view about what arithmetic and elementary mathematics are about. The key idea behind this view is that arithmetic is a *part* of algebra (see Fig. P.2), namely, that part that deals with number systems, the number line, simple functions, and so on. Arithmetic deals with the part of algebra in which particular numbers and measures are treated as instances of more general examples.

Isolated examples can always be treated as instances of something more general. The number 327 stands for $(3 \times 100) + (2 \times 10) + (7 \times 1)$, which is just an instance of the more general expression $(a \times 100) + (b \times 10) + (c \times 1)$, which can be expressed even more generally for an arbitrary radix or base. Opportunities for generalizing, for thinking about functions and variables, and for using algebraic notation, abound in elementary mathematics.

To consider arithmetic as a part of algebra encourages us to view isolated examples and topics as instances of more abstract ideas and concepts. Addition, for example, is a computational method. It is also a function with certain general properties. Likewise multiplication by two is a table of number facts ($1 \times 2 = 2$; $2 \times 2 = 4$; $3 \times 2 = 6$; $4 \times 2 = 8$) and also a function that maps a set of input values to unique output values. The latter idea can be expressed algebraically, for instance, through the mapping notation $x \rightarrow 2x$, the standard notation for functions, $f(x) = 2x$, or the graph on a Cartesian plane of a relation between x and y corresponding to the equation $y = 2x$.

It will help to bear these points in mind while reading the following research chapters. It may first appear that the problems we gave children to solve are arithmetical. On looking more closely, the reader will note their algebraic character. The categories *arithmetical* and *algebraic* are not mutually exclusive.

This does not mean that every idea, concept, and technique from arithmetic is manifestly algebraic; however, each is *potentially* algebraic.[2] Concepts such as equivalence can and should be treated early on in ways consistent with their usage in more advanced mathematics unless there are compelling reasons not to.

That arithmetic is a part of algebra is neither obvious nor trivial, especially for those of us who followed the "arithmetic first, algebra much later" route through our own mathematics education.

RETHINKING OUR VIEWS
ABOUT YOUNG STUDENTS

People from Aristotle's day would likely have considerable difficulty grasping mathematical ideas that a high school student of today can readily comprehend. This is not because today's students are "smarter" or "better at mathematics." The Greeks of antiquity represented problems largely through natural language and geometry. Today's high school stu-

---

[2]On the other hand, not all algebra is generalized arithmetic. Abstract algebras, for instance those that treat the operation of addition as noncommutative (the order of operands matters) or those that describe operations on objects other than numbers, are bona fide examples of nonarithmetical algebra.

dents have access to modern algebraic notation that emerged only in the last handful of centuries (Harper, 1987). Algebraic notation may not "come natural to them" but it ultimately offers important payoffs. Consider the following two expressions of the same proposition:

> If there be any number of magnitudes whatever which are, respectively, equi-multiples of any magnitudes equal in multitude, then, whatever multiple one of the magnitudes is of one, that multiple also will all be of all. (Euclid, 1956, p. 138)

It is difficult to make heads or tails of Euclid's point without the benefits of modern-day symbolic notation. Now look at the "same expression" rendered in symbolic notation:[3]

> Prop. I then asserts that, if ma, mb, mc, etc. be any equimultiples of a, b, c, etc., then $ma + mb + mc + \ldots = m(a + b + c + \ldots)$. (Euclid, 1956, p. 139)

Even "simple" representations such as place value notation and column multiplication were uncommon before 1500. Psychologists and educators may see a developmental pattern in the emergence of concepts such as multiplication, ratio, and proportion—overlooking the fact that students in today's schools are given explicit instruction about these topics from around 9 years of age. The same may hold for algebraic concepts: Given the proper circumstances and learning experiences, students may be capable of learning algebra notation much earlier, as an integral part of early mathematics instruction.

The mathematics education community sorely needs careful analyses of children's understanding of mathematical rules, their own ways of approaching and representing algebra problems in different contexts, and instructional models for initiating algebra instruction. Such research needs to be conducted under special circumstances because typical classrooms make restrictive assumptions about what students are capable of learning.

---

[3]One might think that Expression 1 is merely an awkward translation into English of Heiberg's German translation of Euclid's Greek text—fair enough. However, if that is the case, then the reader should surely be able to rewrite Expression 1 in clear English. We find it highly unlikely that the reader can rewrite Expression 1 with the clarity of Expression 2. The difficulty lies in the fact that the particular magnitudes and multiples cannot be nimbly referred to in natural language.

GOALS OF THIS BOOK

We have been charting children's initial understandings and how their algebraic reasoning evolves as they take part in classroom activities designed to bring to the forefront the potentially algebraic nature of arithmetic and thinking about quantities. Our approach to the study of early algebraic reasoning includes analyses of children's reasoning processes and of classroom activities, with a deep concern with mathematics content, mathematical notation, and the relationship between arithmetic and algebra.

This volume deals with the pressing issues faced by teachers and faculty in teacher preparation programs regarding how to implement the NCTM goals of introducing algebra in the early grades. Through our classroom examples, we demonstrate that this is possible. We also discuss some of the conditions under which it may be achieved.

- Chapter 1 reviews findings about algebraic reasoning and describes our approach to early algebra.
- Chapter 2 looks at how young children make sense of algebraic ideas in different contexts.
- Chapter 3 looks at the notations children produce in solving algebraic problems.
- Chapter 4 focuses on how students reason about addition and subtraction as functions.
- Chapter 5 focuses on how students understand multiplication when it is presented as a function.
- Chapter 6 examines how children use notations in algebraic problems involving fractions.
- Chapter 7 summarizes the findings and draws implications for early mathematics education.

CD-ROM VIDEOPAPERS

To make the case more compelling, we have included on a CD-ROM additional text and video footage for chapters 4 through 6. The three videopapers (written text with embedded video footage) present relevant discussions that help identify students' reasoning. The printed text in the present book includes transcriptions of the video episodes in the CD. It is possible to understand the chapters without the CD-ROM; however, it is strongly recommended that readers watch the video clips before reading the transcription of the episodes. They convey the children's understanding of the tasks we proposed, as well as provide evidence of what children are convinced of, intrigued with, and puzzled by.

To open the videopaper, open your Internet browser and select 'index.html' in the corresponding chapter folder. After a short time, the text will appear on the right side of the page and the video on the left side. As you read the text, you may click on the links marked "start" to play the corresponding video portion. Alternatively, you may simply open the files named Chapter4.mov, Chapter5.mov, or Chapter6.mov and play the QuickTime movie. The movie has subtitles to help you follow the dialogue. The drop-down list of episodes from the right-side bar under the video screen allows you to move from episode to episode.

WHO THIS BOOK IS FOR

For algebra to find a useful place in the early mathematics curriculum, considerable progress needs to be made on matters of possibility (Can young students learn algebra?), desirability (Is it good for them to learn it?), and implementation (How can it be done?).

This book was written especially for educators, researchers, curriculum developers, and graduate students who have wondered whether it is possible for young students to understand algebra. In the findings reported here, we focus on two questions at the heart of algebraic understanding: "Can students handle the logic of transformations on equal amounts?" (chaps. 2 and 3) and "Can they represent and operate on variables?" (chaps. 4 through 6). The evidence suggests that students can understand concepts that were thought out of their reach until they were several years older.

Those who believe there is little purpose to having young students learn algebra may nonetheless be unmoved by the present evidence. To some extent this is understandable; as Hume (1737–1740/2003) rightly noted many years ago, statements about *what ought to happen* cannot be inferred from statements about *what is the case*. Nonetheless, here is where evidence of a different nature may be of help. We have found, time and time again, that young students enjoy solving mathematical problems that are truly challenging. And the video footage on the accompanying CD helps convey their sense of satisfaction and interest.

Practitioners and developers may also glean in the ensuing chapters ideas about how to integrate algebra into the existing mathematics curriculum—not ready-made solutions, but rather new ways of thinking about old topics. For example, chapters 4 and 5 offer ideas on how addition and multiplication can be approached as functions instead of as mere computation routines. Likewise, the conversations between students and adults exemplify how illusive mathematical issues can be discussed in ways that make sense to young students. But by and large, this book is written for those hoping to enter largely uncharted waters of Early Algebra at a time when few if any clear guides exist.

ACKNOWLEDGMENTS

We wish to thank the National Science Foundation (NSF Grants #9722732 and #9909591) and the Conselho Nacional de Desenvolviment Científico e Tecnológico (CNPq-the Brazilian agency for research and scientific development), which have supported our investigations of young children's understanding of algebraic concepts and notations.

Many people contributed to the studies reported here. Susanna Lara-Roth read and carefully commented on each chapter. Darrell Earnest assembled the videopapers for chapters 4 through 6. The *Bridging Research and Practice* project at TERC developed the Videopaper Builder. Thelma Davis graciously opened the doors to her third-grade classroom in Somerville, MA, so we could work with her class of delightful 9-year-olds; Fred O'Meara, then principal at East Somerville Community School, also welcomed us warmly.

We wish to thank Alan Schoenfeld and Lawrence Erlbaum Associates for their support in this project. We realize that the marketplace exerts a strong pressure on publishers to offer books promising to quickly change schools. We believe that one of the most promising ways to change mathematics education for the better is to provide a research basis for curriculum developers and teacher educators in which to craft their own work.

Over the past decades, we have learned from many thinkers and re-searchers in mathematics education. We acknowledge many of them by referring to their work in the chapters that follow. Three people neverthe-less deserve special mention here. Gérard Vergnaud showed us that Piaget left an important legacy for mathematics education; but, in addition to mathematical invariants, one needs to consider symbolic representations and situations. This seemingly simple idea implies that people's conceptu-alizations of mathematical and scientific phenomena are considerably richer and broader than concepts. It also means that researchers of mathe-matical learning have a role in clarifying issues of 'mathematical content' that fall outside the purview of mathematics. We are also grateful for the many insights that Judah Schwartz provided into mathematics and the thinking of the students in our research. Judah showed us that functions deserve a prominent place in early mathematics education. For this pro-posal to work successfully, many topics in the existing curriculum need to be re-conceptualized—from the humble operations of addition and sub-traction [the functions $f(a,b) = a + b$ and $g(a,b) = a - b$] to equations as the setting equal of two functions. Finally, we express thanks to Jim Kaput, who united a variety of people, including ourselves, in far ranging discus-sions about algebraic thinking among young children. With contagious en-thusiasm and provocative ideas, Jim showed that algebra has an important role to play in early mathematics education. With Jim's recent passing, we have lost a very dear friend and colleague.

1

Interpreting Research About Learning Algebra

Most research about algebra learning has focused on students' success and failure. To be sure, it has provided important information on how well students perform at various ages, what they find challenging, and what kinds of errors and misinterpretations they typically make. Researchers' questions and recommendations also provide glimpses into their changing views about algebra, cognitive development, and learning and instruction. The general picture is that algebra has been a "moving target."

In this chapter, we consider findings about performance and then look at various attempts to improving algebra instruction. The presentation is not organized chronologically, but rather in terms of a growing departure from the view that "algebra is just too hard for most students" and from recommendations that we need to focus on a hypothetical "transition stage from arithmetic to algebra," to reserve algebra for gifted students or, in the case of most students, to wait until they are well advanced in mathematics.

STUDENT PERFORMANCE IN ALGEBRA

For many years, the National Assessment of Educational Progress (NAEP) provided a dismal view of student performance in algebra. In 2003, the average rate of success among eighth-grade students on the 17 algebra items made public on the NAEP website was 46%. Students performed much better (72% correct) on items related to number sense and arithmetical operations. These and other results would seem to confirm what most teachers, parents, and students already know: Algebra is not easy. But, is it really the case that young students cannot understand algebra? And, if algebra is so difficult for middle and high school students, why are we proposing to introduce algebra in elementary school?

To address these questions, let us first consider typical students' difficulties with algebra. We then look at the transitional approaches to algebra. We also consider the possibility that children's difficulties are at least partly due to how they have been taught. Then, we review the case for introducing algebra in elementary school and consider what an algebrafied curriculum for the elementary school years might look like.

Research on Students' Initial Difficulties With Algebra

Much of the research on algebra learning has focused on students' errors in manipulating equations. Students begin learning about algebra with a strongly rooted belief that the equals sign (=) represents a unidirectional operator that produces an output on the right side from the input on the left (Booth, 1984; Kieran, 1981, 1985; Vergnaud, 1985, 1988). Moreover, they focus on finding particular answers (Booth, 1984), do not recognize the commutative and distributive properties (Boulton-Lewis, Cooper, Atweh, Pillay, & Wilss, 2001; Demana & Leitzel, 1988; MacGregor, 1996), do not use mathematical symbols to express relationships between quantities (Bednarz, 2001; Bednarz & Janvier, 1996; Vergnaud, 1985; Wagner, 1981), do not comprehend the use of letters as generalized numbers or as variables (Booth, 1984; Kuchemann, 1981; Vergnaud, 1985), have great difficulty operating on unknowns, and fail to understand that equivalent transformations on both sides of an equation do not alter its truth value (Bednarz, 2001; Bednarz & Janvier, 1996; Filloy & Rojano, 1989; Kieran, 1985, 1989; Steinberg, Sleeman, & Ktorza, 1990).

Researchers frequently attributed students' poor performance to shortcomings in their reasoning, often thought to emanate from cognitive–developmental constraints. Collis (1975) and Kucheman (1981), for instance, related students' responses on algebra problems to neo-Piagetian levels of understanding, MacGregor (2001) argued that most students do not benefit from algebra instruction because many of them still are concrete thinkers, and Filloy and Rojano (1989) posited the existence of a historical and individual "cut-point" separating arithmetic thought from algebraic thought—"a break in the development concerning operations on the unknown" (p. 19). This cut-point was offered to help explain why 12- to 13-year-old students were unable to solve first-degree equations with a variable on both sides of the equals sign (e.g., $38x + 72 = 56x$). In a similar vein, Herscovics and Linchevski (1994) argued that many students were unable "to operate spontaneously with or on the unknown" (p. 59).

Sfard and Linchevski (1994) proposed that, historically and ontologically, algebra is first process-oriented and only later the processes become reified and treated as structures or as mathematical objects (see also Sfard, 1995). The expression, $3(x + 5) + 1$ can be legitimately viewed as a computational process, a number, a function, a member of a family of functions, or a string of symbols with no external meaning. According to Sfard and Linchevski, students initially treat expressions as computations, only later conceiving of them as objects that can serve as input for additional, higher order, operations.

THE TRANSITIONAL APPROACH AS A RESPONSE TO STUDENTS' DIFFICULTIES

Because it was commonly assumed that young students did not possess the cognitive wherewithal to learn algebra, it appeared reasonable to maintain the onset of algebra instruction at adolescence and to use the period immediately preceding Algebra 1 for preparing students for what was to come. Transitional, pre-algebra approaches were developed with the aim of helping students make a smooth transition from pre-algebraic mathematics to algebra. Early transitional approaches focused on helping students solve equations. Subsequent approaches took a broader view of algebra.

Focus on Equations

Herscovics and Kieran (1980) addressed seventh and eighth graders' limited interpretation of the equals sign as an operator (see Kieran, 1985a) in an intervention based on the expansion of students' notion of equality and the gradual transformation of arithmetic expressions into algebraic equations. Six weeks after the beginning of the intervention, the authors concluded that the six participants in the study showed a "clear understanding of arithmetical identities, equations, and algebraic rules" (Herscovics & Kieran, 1980, p. 579). Vergnaud (1988) and Vergnaud, Cortes, and Favre-Artigue (1988) took seventh- to ninth-grade students at risk of failing in algebra courses through a series of activities based on the behavior of a two-plate balance scale. The problems were resistant to solution through numerical computation and, thus, seemed to require algebraic methods. Students initially worked on problems in symbolic form with a variable appearing on only one side of the equals sign. Later problems were introduced with variables on both sides. According to Filloy and Rojano (1989), these were problems from the more difficult side of the "cognitive gap." The researchers established a didactical contract with students to encourage them to use algebra manipulation methods to find a solution. By the end of the study, a dramatic reversal had taken place. The at-risk students were performing better than their peers on algebra problems that required generating equations from word problems and then solving them through conventional symbolic methods and syntactic rules. Filloy and Rojano (1989) themselves were less successful in their attempt to bridge the gap between arithmetic and algebra through work with geometrical and balance scale models aimed at promoting use of syntactic rules for solving equations. They found the students disinclined to adopt algebraic methods and required constant intervention by the teacher to do so.

Such apparently conflicting results might seem to suggest that nothing clear can be concluded. Granted, it is difficult to isolate causal factors in successful interventions. However, successful studies expose as inadequate the idea that cognitive–developmental constraints are to blame for the poor performance in algebra of a large proportion of students.

Students' difficulties may reflect how they have been taught: In elementary school, the equals sign (=) is generally introduced as a unidirectional operator corresponding to the notion of "makes" or "yields." Students are told they cannot subtract a larger number from a smaller one, multiplication is the same as repeated addition, and that some nonzero integers cannot be divided by others. There is a heavy emphasis in arithmetic instruction on obtaining numerical answers to operations involving particular numbers and measures. When letters are finally introduced as symbols for variables, they are misunderstood as placeholders for particular numbers. These are all examples of instructional blunders that have been institutionalized in early mathematics curricula and practice. They are blunders in that they encourage students to think about mathematics in a shortsighted way. In the long term, they will need to be replaced.

There is not much relief to be found by plucking out and crushing each blunder one at a time. Rather, the field of early mathematics education needs coherent, long-term alternatives to current approaches that make sense both mathematically and pedagogically.

Expanding Transitional Approaches to Algebra

Over time, researchers have moved away from equation solving as the ultimate goal of algebra instruction. Accordingly, transitional approaches switched from exclusive focus on equations to work involving generalization, number patterns, variables, and functions.

Bednarz (2001) attempted to stimulate the emergence and development of algebraic procedures among 13- to 14-year-olds in a problem-solving context by stressing mathematical generalization and the representation of number patterns. Students first dealt with arithmetical comparison problems and later were encouraged to solve algebra problems focusing on mathematical generalization and comparisons. Bednarz' preliminary results suggest that students' written responses, which often included intermediate notations (such as verbal descriptions and iconic representations of quantities), are important transitional tools that help them find solutions to algebra problems. Fujii and Stephens (2001) proposed that quasi-variables can serve as a convenient bridge between arithmetic and algebraic thinking. As they explain, quasi-variables, commonly used in Japanese elementary school mathematics, appear "in a number sentence or group of number sentences that indicate an underlying mathematical relationship which remains true whatever the numbers used are" (p. 259). For example, the sentence $78 - 49 + 49 = 78$ belongs to the class of formal algebraic expressions of the type $a - b + b = a$, which is true for any values of a, b. According to Fujii and Stephens, work with quasi-variables would assist children in identifying and discussing algebraic generalizations long before they learn formal algebraic notation. Although these are promising proposals, they do not explore the possibility that young children might learn to use algebraic notation itself.

Transitional approaches to algebra as the study of variables and functions have often call for the use of computers for bridging arithmetic and algebra.

Logo was often advocated as an environment for mathematical learning, particularly in the case of algebra and geometry (Hoyles & Noss, 1992; Papert, 1980). Ursini (1994, 1997, 2001) used Logo as an informal environment in which children explored the notion of variable as a generalized number, as a specific unknown, and as a functional relationship, before being immersed in more formal contexts. Through workshops and guidance from peers and teachers, 12- and 13-year-olds switch from a focus on the static relationship between two quantities to considering the dynamic aspects relating two quantities and how the two quantities change in a functional relationship. However, data also show that learning to program in Logo does not guarantee that one will understand variables and functions (Healy, Hoyles, & Sutherland, 1990; Ursini, 1994, 1997, 2001). The activities would need to be specially structured and aimed at encouraging students to move from specific arithmetic representations to general representations of an algebraic nature.

Computer spreadsheets have also been used as a means for introducing students to algebra. Sutherland and Rojano (1993; see also Rojano, 1996, and Sutherland, 1993) found that, from age 10, Mexican and U.K. students with training in spreadsheet activities performed relatively well in algebraic tasks. At the beginning of their study, children in both samples preferred to use nonalgebraic approaches, working from known amounts to calculate the unknown amounts. As they worked with spreadsheets, they progressed towards using algebraic strategies, working with the unknown quantity in the problem and operating on it as if it were known.

Over the last few years, an increasing number of software environments have been created to specifically address the teaching and learning of variables and functions. Kieran, Boileau, and Garançon (1996) proposed that the intermediary representations the students use as they work with computer software offer links to conventional representations. Heid (1996) described how algebraic thinking emerges as students are introduced to algebra via computer technology that allows them to model real-world situations. Schwartz (1995) considered functions as the basic mathematical object and the core of algebra and argued that computer technology can affect students' schooling by deepening and broadening understanding, providing a conceptual grounding for manipulative skills, and inviting conjecture and exploration. Multiple Software environments by Schwartz (1995, 1996) and Schwartz and Yerushalmy (1991, 1992a, 1992b, 1995) highlight the fact that there are multiple ways in which to represent mathematical situations and allow students to use different kinds of representations—symbolic language, numerical language, graphical language, and natural language—with agility. The software becomes a tool for modeling situations and relationships and a medium for students to re-represent their understandings and to flexibly move among the different kinds of representations.

The potential of the functions approach to algebra is undeniable. Still, as was the case with other approaches and tools, we are far from the wide implementation and evaluation of students' learning through the proposed activities. Interestingly, even though many of the authors just cited recognized that part of the problem lay in children's previous experiences with arithmetic, with rare exception did they question the traditional curriculum sequence of arithmetic first, algebra later.

A MORE RADICAL APPROACH: INTRODUCE ALGEBRA IN ELEMENTARY SCHOOL

To help students make a smooth transition from arithmetic to algebra seems reasonable enough. However, the view that algebra has an important role to fulfill in the early mathematics curriculum has become increasingly widespread among researchers and policymakers. In the 1960s, Davis (1967, 1971/1972, 1985, 1989) proposed that preparation for algebra should begin in Grades 2 or 3. Vergnaud (1988) suggested that algebra or pre-algebra should start at the elementary school level. Davydov (1991) argued that algebra, including algebraic notation, be taught from Grade 1. Mason (1996) forcefully promoted a focus on generalization at the elementary school level. Kaput (1998) emphatically argued that the weaving of algebra throughout the K–12 curriculum could lend coherence, depth, and power to school mathematics, and replace late, abrupt, isolated, and superficial high-school algebra courses. And Schoenfeld (1998), reporting on the conclusions of one of the Algebra Initiative Colloquium Working Groups (Lacampagne, 1995), proposed that algebra should pervade the curriculum instead of appearing in isolated courses in middle or high school. In the Proceedings of the 12th ICMI Study Conference on the Future of the Teaching and Learning of Algebra (Chick, Stacey, Vincent, & Vincent, 2001), an overwhelming call for the integration of arithmetic and algebra in the early grades was witnessed (see Brown & Coles, 2001; Crawford, 2001; Henry, 2001; Warren, 2001). The claim for algebra in elementary school became so influential that the NCTM in its 2000 Principles and Standards for School Mathematics (NCTM, 2000) came to endorse the idea that algebraic reasoning should be nurtured from kindergarten and that algebra notation should be part of the elementary school curriculum from Grade 3.

Why would such a large number of researchers, mathematics educators, and policymakers embrace the idea of introducing algebra in the early grades, when students presumably should be learning arithmetic and number facts?

Let's look closely at the rationale for introducing algebra from the first years of elementary school: To proponents of early algebra, early mathematics (especially arithmetic) and algebra are not fully distinct. They would argue, for example, that a deep understanding of arithmetic requires certain mathematical generalizations. Some would argue further that algebraic notation would make it easier for both adults and young learners to give expression to such mathematical generalizations (Brizuela, 2004; Carraher, Schliemann, & Brizuela, 1999, 2000). Several years ago Booth (1988) stated that:

> . . . algebra is not separate from arithmetic; indeed, it is in many respects 'generalized arithmetic.' And herein lies the source of other difficulties. To appreciate the generalization of arithmetical relationships and procedures requires first that those relationships and procedures be apprehended within the arithmetical context. If they are not recognized, or if students have misconceptions concerning them, then this may well affect the students' performance in algebra. In this event, the difficulties that students experience in algebra are not so much difficulties in algebra itself as problems in arithmetic that remains uncorrected. (p. 29)

One of Davydov's collaborators actually suggests that "the algebraic method is the more effective and more 'natural' way of solving problems with the aid of equations in mathematics" than the arithmetical method (Bodanskii, 1991, p. 276).

The question still under debate is: Can young students really deal with algebra? In recent years, researchers, teacher-developers, and theorists have begun to examine how young children understand algebraic concepts and representations. We describe some of these empirical analyses in the following section as a first step towards examining the feasibility of introducing algebra in elementary school.

YOUNG CHILDREN DOING ALGEBRA

One of the clearest demonstrations that children can and should start learning algebra in elementary school comes from the classroom studies by Davydov's team in the former Soviet Union (see Davydov, 1991). Bodanskii's results (1991) constitute a compelling example of their successful approach with children who received instruction on the algebraic representation of verbal problems from Grades 1 to 4. Children in the experimental group used algebraic notation to solve verbal problems and performed better than their control peers throughout the school years. At the end of fourth grade, when compared to sixth and seventh graders in traditional programs of 5 years of arithmetic followed by algebra instruction from Grade 6, they also showed better performance in algebra problem solving.

More recently, Brito Lima (1996; see also Brito Lima & da Rocha Falcão, 1997) showed that first- to sixth-grade Brazilian children can develop written representations for algebraic problems and, with help from the interviewer, solve linear equation problems using different solution strategies. Other promising results come from Lins Lessa's (1995) work with fifth graders (11- to 12-year-olds) in Brazil. She found that after only one individual teaching session, the children could solve verbal problems or situations presented on a balance scale corresponding to equations such as $x + y + 70 = 2x + y + 20$. Their solutions were based on the development of written equations and, in more than 60% of the cases, on the use of algebra syntactic rules for solving equations.

Evidence that elementary school children can reason algebraically has been building up over the years in U.S. classrooms as a result of the implementation of reform curriculum in mathematics education. Carpenter and Levi (2000) and Carpenter and Franke (2001) showed fairly young children (who participated in classroom activities that explore mathematical relations through the use of number sentences) talking meaningfully about the truth or falsity of issues such as, "Is it true that $a + b - b = a$ for any numbers a and b?" In classrooms where reasoning about mathematical relations is the focus of instruction, Schifter (1999) found compelling examples of implicit algebraic reasoning and generalizations by elementary school children. As she described it:

> Algebraic methods are clearly implicit in the children's work. . . . As they apply different operations to solve a single word problem, they evidence a sense of how the operations are related. For example, as the children come to see that any missing-addend problem can be solved by subtraction, or that any division problem can be solved by finding the missing factor, they acquire experience with the inverse relationships of addition and subtraction, multiplication and division, and thus with equivalent equations. And as they develop fluency in a variety of computational strategies, they implicitly apply the laws of commutativity, associativity, and distributivity. (p. 75)

Blanton and Kaput (2000) further showed third graders' ability to make robust generalizations and to provide intuitive supporting arguments as they discussed operations on even and odd numbers and considered them as placeholders or as variables. Other examples of young children's algebraic reasoning and use of algebra notation are found in Ainley (1999), Bellisio and Maher (1998), Slavitt (1999), and Smith (2000).

Studies on young children's understanding and representation of functions and variables, though, are rather scarce. One exception is the work by Davis (1967, 1971/1972), who developed a series of classroom activities to introduce concepts and notation for variables, Cartesian coordinates, and functions in elementary and middle school. These tasks were successfully piloted in Grades 5 to 9 and, as Davis proposed, many of the activities would be appropriate for children from Grade 2 onwards.

The studies just discussed clearly support the view that algebra students' difficulties in algebra may have been due to the shortcomings of instruction. The studies show that children can successfully learn about the rules and principles of algebra equations in the early grades. At the same time, they bring to the surface the need for researchers to look closely at children's discussions and reasoning processes (as they participate in classroom activities or interviews) to identify students' learning processes and how they deal with patterns, generalization, and functions. However, systematic data on how young children responded to the tasks are still missing in the early algebra literature. Hopefully, this book contributes to filling this gap.

OUR APPROACH

For many years students' difficulties with algebra were seen as a matter of cognitive development. However, a closer look at research data and at the traditional mathematics curriculum points to students' previous experience with arithmetic as a more plausible source of typical mistakes. We believe that their difficulties stem largely from:

- A reliance on restricted problem sets (e.g. emphasis on change problems with few comparisons and missing addend problems in early arithmetic);
- A focus on notation as a means for registering computations rather than for providing a description of what is known about a problem;
- A focus on computation of particular set of values rather than on relations among sets.

We do not deny that there are developmental constraints to learning. We suggest, however, that students' difficulties are accentuated and prolonged by the stark separation between arithmetic and algebra. This separation cannot be adequately handled by programs designed to ease the transition from arithmetic to algebra, but requires that they be integrated, where possible, from the very start. The contrast between children's difficulties with algebra in high school and successful attempts to teach algebra at earlier grades further supports the view that it is time to seriously consider deep changes in the elementary mathematics curriculum and the possibility of having children discussing, understanding, and dealing with algebraic concepts and relations much earlier than is the norm nowadays. But where and how should we start?

Bodanskii's (1991) study is a good start, but leaves unanswered many questions concerning children's understanding of algebraic procedures, especially in what concerns the understanding of the rules for transforming equations, functions, and variables.

The studies by Carpenter and Levi (2000), by Carpenter and Franke (2001), and by Schifter (1999), point to the natural integration between arithmetical and algebraic understandings but do not deal with algebraic representation. The same is true for studies that focus on algebra as generalization.

We believe that many of the notational tools used in arithmetic can be presented in new ways. In traditional arithmetic, the equals sign (=) is often interpreted as the unidirectional "gives" or "yields"; in the algebraic universe of discourse equality is a bi-directional statement. Similarly, in traditional arithmetic the plus sign (+) is restricted to the idea of joining or increasing amounts, whereas, in algebra, it is often used where no such actions or events occur. Operators can and should be explored in arithmetical settings in a broader manner.

We have been exploring how this might be achieved with regard to addition, subtraction, multiplication, and division. We believe there are good reasons for treating arithmetical operations as functions in early mathematics instruction and we spend the main part of this book clarifying our view and exploring examples of how this could be achieved.

Our approach to the introduction of algebraic concepts and notations in elementary school is guided by the ideas that:

- Arithmetical operations can be viewed as functions;
- Generalizing lies at the heart of algebraic reasoning;
- We should provide students with opportunities to use letters to stand for unknown amounts and for variables.

We focus here on algebra as a generalized arithmetic of numbers and quantities. Accordingly, we view the introduction of algebraic activities in elementary school as a move from thinking about relations among particular numbers and measures toward thinking about relations among sets of numbers and measures, from computing numerical answers to describing relations among variables. Children need to be aware that, as Schoenfeld and Arcavi (1988) emphasized, "a variable varies" (p. 421). This requires providing a series of problems to students, so that they can begin to note and articulate the general patterns they see among variables. Tables play a crucial role in this process because they allow one to systematically register diverse outcomes (one per row) and look for patterns in the results. Algebraic notation, even at the early grades, is also fundamental as a tool to represent multiple possible values and to understanding relationships between two sets of variables.

We hope that the set of interview and classroom data discussed in the following chapters will support our claim that algebra can become part of the elementary mathematics curriculum and that the many difficulties students have with algebra are exacerbated by the restrictive approach to arithmetic presently practiced in most schools.

Furthermore, we believe that mathematical understanding is an individual construction that is transformed and expanded through social interaction, experience in meaningful contexts, and access to cultural systems and cultural tools. When psychologists evaluate the "development" of children who have already entered school, they are not dealing directly with cognitive universals. In attempting to fully understand the development of mathematical reasoning, we need analyses of how children learn as they (a) participate in cultural practices, (b) interact with teachers and peers in the classroom, (c) become familiar with mathematical symbols and tools, and (d) deal with mathematics across a variety of situations. The teaching and learning of mathematics as a discipline unfolds from children's basic logical and mathematical understandings, leading to more general, complex, and explicit knowledge. To acknowledge this, however, is not enough. We need to analyze how children's initial logical and mathematical understandings can be further expanded as they participate in instructional activities. Ultimately we need to find "the most adequate methods for bridging the transition between . . . natural but non-reflective structures to conscious reflection upon such structures and to a theoretical formulation of them" (Piaget, 1970a, p. 47).

I

INTERVIEW STUDIES

As we described in chapter 1, the field of mathematics education has gradually embraced the idea that algebra need not be postponed until adolescence. Many researchers and educators now believe that elementary algebraic ideas and notation should be an integral part of young students' understanding of early mathematics. The contrast between children's difficulties with algebra in high school and a few successful attempts to teach algebra at earlier grades suggests that it is time to seriously consider deep changes in the elementary mathematics curriculum and the possibility of having children discussing and dealing with algebraic concepts, relations, and representations much earlier than is the norm nowadays.

However, can elementary school children really understand the logico-mathematical relations implicit in algebraic rules? Can they develop and understand ways of approaching and representing algebra problems? What are the most adequate instructional models for initiating algebra instruction? As we started our early algebra studies, little was known about elementary school children's understanding of algebraic principles, notation, and procedures. We chose to start with interview studies that would give us a first look at children's potential in terms of understanding algebraic principles.

Building on research findings about cognitive performance across contexts and the potential role of representational tools in reasoning, the two interview studies described in the first part of this book look at children's understanding of a basic algebraic principle across different contexts (chap. 2 and part of chap. 3) and examine children's intuitive use of notation to solve algebraic problems (chap. 3).

Young Children's Understanding of Equivalences

Analúcia D. Schliemann
Monica Lins Lessa
Anna Paula Brito Lima
Alane Siqueira

As we started considering the cognitive challenges children face as they learn algebra, our question was: Do young children understand that equal transformations performed on equal amounts do not change its truth-value? For instance, when would children be able to see that if two players have the same unknown amounts of marbles and each player loses three marbles, one would still have the same amount as the other? Under what conditions would they understand that basic rule? Would they see that this is true for amounts they can count as well as for mathematical equations? What about verbal problems and equalities on a balance scale? Do they always need to know the specific amounts with which they are dealing? Do they need to compute the final values in the comparison to state that the equality remains? Or, can they solve the problem based on pure logic?

As we pointed out in chapter 1, previous research suggests that this fundamental logical principle underlying rules for solving equations is difficult to grasp even by adolescents (e.g., Filloy & Rojano, 1989). We believe, however, that the difficulties and mistakes found among adolescents learning algebra result from arithmetic instruction rather than from a cognitive inability to deal with transformations on equalities.

When a woodworker cuts a set of bookshelves out of a wood board, there is an invariance between the amounts of wood before and after the work is done (if one remembers to consider the shavings and scraps on the workshop floor). However, this fact does not necessarily express the woodworker's view. He may think of his action as exerting a unidirectional effect: The board becomes a set of shelves, but the inverse does not hold. In this view, the initial boards of wood and the resulting shelves are not equivalent. Classroom observations and research on students' difficulties with algebra suggest that arithmetic instruction encourages students to think about mathematical operations like the woodworker thinks about his actions on raw wood. The student receives givens that must be transformed through a series of one-way operations into output or *answers*. The initial state is fundamentally different from the final state. For example, one begins with a certain amount of money, spends some, and then has less. Such characterizations suggest that number sentences describe how one gets from one state (more money) to another, different state (less money). This may lead to the common interpretation of the equals sign (=) as meaning *gives* or *yields*.

After years of arithmetic problem solving, when students are finally introduced to algebra, the meaning of equivalence, operations, and equations needs to undergo a sudden paradigm shift. Whereas in arithmetic, the given operations corresponded to the calculations the student was expected to carry out, things change in algebra. Operations are now meant to describe logical relations among elements (quantities or variables). In an expression such as "$a^2 - b^2$" the minus sign indicates a subtraction and yet, in algebra, one may be expected to factor or reorganize the equation and not necessarily to perform the subtraction. *Equals* no longer means *produces* or *gives*. Equations in algebra become a major and challenging activity in high school.

One of the basic rules for solving simple equations is expressed as "when you move one element from one side of the equation to the other side you have to change its sign." This rule is a shortcut for making equal additive transformations on both sides of the equation. But, do students realize that adding or subtracting equal unknowns from each expression will not alter the equality? Research results show that this logical principle does not spontaneously guide high school students' solutions when they try to solve equations. Students' typical mistakes with simple equations (see Kieran, 1985, 1989) seem to reflect a failure to understand that equivalent transformations on both sides of an equation do not alter the equality. Even 13- to 15-year-old students who were asked whether two linear equations had the same solution (for instance, $x + 2 = 5$ and $x + 2 - 2 = 5 - 2$) rarely justified their answers by appealing to the idea of equal operations on the left and right expressions (Steinberg, Sleeman, & Ktorza, 1990). Instead, they choose to work out values for the unknown in each of the equations and to compare their results at the end. Resnick, Cauzinille-Marmeche, and Mathieu (1987) described similar results for 11- to 14-year-old French pupils.

Why do students not take into account such an apparently simple logical rule? Are they unable to understand it? Is their difficulty specifically linked to the written representation of equalities with symbolic notation? Or does it also appear when they deal with physical models to represent equivalence or with their own spontaneous methods to solve verbal problems?

CONTEXTS FOR UNDERSTANDING EQUIVALENCE

Resnick, Cauzinille-Marmeche, and Mathieu (1987) advocated for grounding algebra instruction in referential meaning as a way to promote understanding of the linkage between situations and algebraic formalism, a necessary condition for the use of algebra to solve problems. Two-pan balance scales have been widely used as a physical device to provide meaning to equations in didactical situations (e.g., Cortes, Kavafian, & Vergnaud, 1990; Filloy & Rojano, 1984, 1989; Vergnaud, Cortes, & Favre-Artigue, 1987) or to analyze the understanding of equalities and manipulation of unknowns among street sellers (Carraher & Schliemann, 1987) and among children (Schliemann, 2000; Schliemann, Brito-Lima, & Santiago, 1992).

In a previous study, we investigated whether 5- to 12-year-old children understood that the equilibrium of a two-pan balance scale is preserved if one removes objects of the same weight from each pan (see Schliemann, Brito-Lima, & Santiago, 1992). We interviewed 80 children (10 of each age level) from a Brazilian private school in Recife, Brazil.

Children were shown a two-pan scale in equilibrium with small labeled weights and/or cereal bags of unknown weights on the two plates. They were told that bags holding the same type of cereals weighed the same. For each item, after obtaining the child's agreement that the total weight on one side of the scale was equal to the total weight on the other side, we asked each child to predict whether the scale would remain in equilibrium if equal bags of nonidentified weights were taken away from each plate, and to explain their predictions. For example, in one of the situations, cereal bags with rice (x), beans (y), and tapioca (z) appeared on the plates of the scale so that $y + x = x + x + z$. Children were asked to judge whether the balance would remain in equilibrium if a bag of rice were to be taken away from each plate. The interview results show that 7- to 10-year-old children recognize that the equality is preserved if equal transformations take place on both sides of the scale. But they reached this conclusion through computation of the values in each pan, or through comparisons between the specific weights to remain on the scale if the proposed transformations would occur. Only 11-year-old children approached the task from a logical point of view, stating that if the weight on one side was equal to the weight on the other—and the same amount was to be subtracted or added from each side—then the remaining weights on the two sides had to be equal.

Younger children's failure in providing logical justifications, however, could be specific to comparisons on a scale and not a general inability to understand the situation as one of logical necessity. The scale in itself may not be well understood (see Booth, 1987) and the fact that the comparison being made refers to weight may constitute an obstacle for children to display their logical understanding (see Piaget & Inhelder, 1962).

We also have to be aware that, although two-platter scales provide a meaningful situation to promote and analyze initial understanding of equations and of rules for algebraic manipulation, they cannot provide a complete model for algebra. For instance, subtraction can be represented through action in the scale, but not as a relation involving two quantities. Multiplication, division, and the concept of variable are difficult, if not impossible, to be represented through the scale model. Furthermore, the presence of numbers and of concrete objects that children could refer to may have constituted an invitation for them to perform computations and to establish direct comparisons between the objects on the scale.

The considerations just described call for studies of children's understanding of equivalences not only in physical models dealing with weight, but also in other models where the comparisons and transformations deal with, for instance, the number of objects or situations where no physical objects are provided. For younger children, a more adequate and accessible substitute for the two-pan balance scale could be the comparison between number of counters such as beads, marbles, or tokens. Another relevant context for the analysis of children's understanding of equivalence is that of verbal problems that refer to physical quantities but are to be solved in the absence of physical referents. Finally, because our main concern relates to the teaching of algebra, written equations should be explored if we want to provide a broad and relevant analysis of children's understanding of the maintenance of equivalence despite transformations.

As is widely known, cognitive performance may considerably vary across contexts. For example, children who fail in Piagetian conservation, class inclusion, or perspective-taking tasks demonstrate logical reasoning when interviewers ask the questions in slightly altered ways (Donaldson, 1978; Light, Buckingham, & Robbins, 1979; McGarrigle & Donaldson, 1974). Across contexts, children may also perform differently in multicausal reasoning (Ceci & Bronfenbrenner, 1985; see also Ceci, 1990, 1993), syllogistic reasoning (Dias & Harris, 1988), and even microlevel cognitive strategies, such as the temporal calibration of one's psychological clock (Ceci & Bronfenbrenner, 1985). It is now fairly widely accepted that specific contexts, far from being incidental, are essential to what is learned and thought.

The contextual nature of cognition, widely recognized in studies of logical reasoning, is also clear when it comes to the analysis of mathematical reasoning. For instance, what children seem to be able to do in formal interview or testing contexts may be rather different from what they may do in informal, out-of-school contexts (Carraher, Carraher, & Schliemann, 1985). Mathematical thinking does not manifest itself invariably across different contexts. The contexts, social goals, and values associated with activities appear to highlight different relations and evoke different approaches and representations. Children draw from the particular social and physical activities in which they engage (e.g., buying and selling, comparing, measuring, computing and solving mathematical problems in and out of school, etc.). Their ways of conceiving and doing mathematics owe much to the specific representations and tools they learn to use in these activities, such as the abacus, weights and measures, quantities, notational systems, and so on (Hatano, 1982; Nunes, Schliemann, & Carraher, 1993).

Given the influence of context on children's display of logical reasoning and mathematical understanding (Carraher, Carraher, & Schliemann, 1985, 1987; Nunes, Schliemann, & Carraher, 1993; Schliemann & Acioly, 1989), we expected that children who fail to provide logical justifications for the preservation of equalities in the balance scale might be able to do so if questions refer to equalities between number of counters. We were not sure what to expect in verbal problems and in equations contexts. Could young children deal with these more abstract contexts? If so, what types of justifications would they produce?

We examined, across different physical models and contexts, how 7- to 12-year-old children come to understand that if one adds or subtracts equal amounts from each side of an equality, the equality remains. The problem items were presented in a fixed order within each context, starting with items where all numerical values under comparison were displayed, followed by items that included partial numerical information, and finally by items with no numerical values whatsoever. By adopting this order, the children's familiarity with numerical values would provide the necessary scaffold for them to consider the items with no numerical values. We expected that, when all the numerical values were known, children would rely on computation to determine whether the equality would remain after the proposed transformations. As the numerical support was reduced and, later, completely eliminated, we expected that children would continue to produce correct answers, but with increasing justifications based on logical principles instead of justifications based on numerical computation.

PARTICIPANTS AND INTERVIEW QUESTIONS

We individually interviewed 120 upper-middle class 7- to 11-year-old Brazilian children. There were 24 children in each age group.

The interviews referred to four contexts, each of them including 16 different items. The four contexts were:

1. Equivalence between weights in a two-pan balance scale;
2. Equivalence between quantities of discrete concrete objects;
3. Equivalence between quantities included in verbal problems; and
4. Equivalence between the two sides of written equations.

Each child was asked to answer all the items in two of the four tasks, in one of the following orders: ab, ac, ad, ba, bc, bd, ca, cb, cd, da, db, and dc. The tasks in each of these orders were presented to a total of 10 children, two in each age group. The 16 items in each one of the four tasks were thus responded by a total of 60 children, 12 from each age group.

Each task/context referred to the same 16 items (see Table 2.1) in terms of structure; what varied was their mode of presentation.

For each of the 16 items, the initial situation of equality was established and the child was asked whether the equality would remain if similar or dissimilar quantities were to be added to or subtracted from the two compared amounts. After answering each item, children were asked to explain their answers. The 16 items and the suggested changes for each task are shown in Table 2.1. In Items 1, 2, 3, 4, and 6, if the suggested changes were to be performed, all the numerical values of the amounts to be compared would be known; in Items 5, 7, 8, 9, 10, and 12, the numerical values would be partially known; in Items 11, 13, 14, 15, and 16, no numerical values would be known if the proposed changes were performed.

TABLE 2.1
Items Included in Each Context

Item	Initial Situation		Suggested Changes		Cardinality of Results
	Side A	Side B	Side A	Side B	
1.	$10 + 2$	$5 + 5 + 2$	subtract 2	subtract 2	Known
2.	7	7	add 6	add 3	Known
3.	$6 + 4$	$3 + 3 + 4$	subtract 6	subtract 3	Known
4.	8	$4 + 4$	add 2	add 2	Known
5.	x	x	add 6	add 3	Partially known
6.	$x + 10$	$x + 5 + 5$	subtract x	subtract x	Known
7.	8	$4 + 4$	add x	add x	Partially known
8.	$x + 6$	$x + 3 + 3$	subtract 6	subtract 3	Partially known
9.	x	$y + y$	add 2	add 2	Partially known
10.	7	7	add x	add y	Partially known
11.	$x + 2$	$y + y + 2$	subtract 2	subtract 2	None known
12.	$x + 2$	$y + y + 2$	subtract x	subtract y	Partially known
13.	$x + z$	$y + y + z$	subtract z	subtract z	None known
14.	$x + z$	$y + y + z$	subtract x	subtract y	None known
15.	z	z	add x	add y	None known
16.	x	$y + y$	add z	add z	None known

The children were given the items in each task in the sequence shown in Table 2.1. The interview followed the principles of the Piagetian clinical method where the child was asked to provide answers and justifications and, whenever necessary, the examiner presented counterarguments to elicit clearer explanations from the part of the child. Paper and pencil were available throughout the interviews for children to use whenever they wanted to.

The Tasks

Task A—Equivalence Between Weights in a Two-Pan Balance Scale. For each one of the 16 items of this task, small labeled weights and boxes of unknown weights were put on the plates of a two-pan scale so that it was in equilibrium (see schematic examples in Figs. 2.1 and 2.2).

The examiner explained to the child that, although the weights of the boxes were not known, boxes of the same color weighed the same. For each item, after obtaining the child's agreement that the total weight on one side of the scale was equal to the total weight on the other side, the examiner asked what would happen if one of the transformations were to be performed. Would the scale remain in equilibrium or not? Following a response, the examiner asked the child to provide a justification to why he or she thought the scale would remain balanced or unbalanced after the proposed transformations.

Task B—Equivalence Between Quantities of Discrete Concrete Objects. For each item of this task, two sets of boxes containing marbles were shown to the child. Some of the boxes were open, so that the child could count

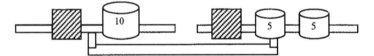

FIG. 2.1.   Scale in equilibrium as in item 16: $x + 10 = x + 5 + 5$.

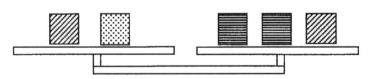

FIG. 2.2.   Scale in equilibrium as in item 13: $x + z = y + y + z$.

how many marbles were in each of them. Others were closed and one couldn't count the number of marbles they held. It was explained to the child that boxes of the same color contained the same number of marbles. For each item, after obtaining the child's agreement that the total number of marbles in one side was equal to the total number in the other side, the examiner asked what would happen if one of the transformations were to be performed. Would the two sides have the same number of marbles or not? Following the child's response, the examiner asked for an explanation for why the number of marbles would remain the same or not.

Task C—Equivalence Between Quantities Included in Verbal Problems. In each one of the items of this task, the examiner presented a verbal problem narrated as a story where two people were described as having, after some events took place, the same number of objects. As a result of a new series of narrated events, equal or different quantities of objects were added or taken away from the previous equivalent amounts. The child was then asked whether the two protagonists of the story still had the same amount of objects. The following are two examples of the verbal problems we presented to children (items 1 and 16):

Bruno and Tiago love to eat chocolate. One day, Bruno took 10 chocolate bars to school and then bought two more at the school store. Tiago brought five chocolate bars to school, then bought five more in the school store, and later got two more from a friend. They had the same number of chocolate bars. During break time, Tiago ate two of his chocolate bars and Bruno also ate two of his chocolate bars. Now, do you think that after the break Tiago has the same number of chocolate bars as Bruno? Or, do you think one has more chocolate bars than the other?

Renata and Claudia collected printed cards. Renata had the same number of cards as Claudia did. Renata had all her cards in one folder. Claudia kept her cards in two folders. Their aunt gave each one of them a new folder with the same number of new cards. Do you think that now Renata has the same number of cards as Claudia? Or do you think that one of them has more cards than the other?

Task D—Equivalence Between the Two Sides of Written Equations. For this task, the child received a sheet of paper with 16 written equations (see Table 2.2). The examiner explained that same letters indi-

TABLE 2.2
The 16 Written Equations

$$10 + 2 = 5 + 5 + 2$$
$$7 = 7$$
$$6 + 4 = 3 + 3 + 4$$
$$8 = 4 + 4$$
$$x = x$$
$$x + 10 = x + 5 + 5$$
$$8 = 4 + 4$$
$$x + 6 = x + 3 + 3$$
$$x = y + y$$
$$7 = 7$$
$$x + 2 = y + y + 2$$
$$x + 2 = y + y + 2$$
$$x + z = y + y + z$$
$$x + z = y + y + z$$
$$z = z$$
$$x = y + y$$

cated equal quantities. For each equation, the child was first asked to judge whether the quantities listed on one side of the equal sign was the same as the quantity on the other side. Following the child's answer that the two quantities were equal, the examiner asked whether they would remain equal if certain numbers or letters in the equation were taken away, or if other numbers or letters were included.

CHILDREN'S ANSWERS ACROSS AGES AND CONTEXTS

Children's Answers and Justifications

The first question that concerned us was: How early would children display an understanding that adding or subtracting equal unknowns to/from each side of an equality will not alter the equality, or that adding or subtracting different unknowns to/from each side of an equality will not preserve the equality?

Our analysis of children's answers to whether the compared amounts would remain equal after transformations showed, to our surprise, that even 7-year-olds gave correct answers to nearly all questions in all four contexts.

Only 2% (81 out of 3,840) of the answers to this initial question were wrong. Moreover, as we see next, even 7-year-olds eventually provided logical justifications to their answers.

Each child's justification to each of the items was classified into one of five categories: unclear, computation, final state, transformation, and logical justification.

Unclear.   In this category we included wrong answers, tautological, and nonrelevant justifications, and missing cases.

Computation.   In this case the child computed the final values of the compared amounts to justify the answers that the amounts would remain equal or would be different after the transformations. When all values to be compared were known, this was a straightforward computation. When some or all values under comparison were unknown, children attributed a number to the unknowns and then proceeded with computations to justify their answer. For example, after answering Item 9 on the equivalence between quantities of concrete objects, one of the children (#46) explained: "Because here (points to the two boxes of same color, on one side of the equality), for instance, there are 2 and 2, that will make 4. And here (pointing to the box of a different color on the other side) it already has 4. Four plus 2 makes 6 and here 4 plus 2 makes 6."

Final State.   Here, the children described or compared the elements that would be left if the proposed transformations were performed. The justification of a child (#37) for Item 11 on the equivalence between weights on a two-pan balance scale exemplifies this type of answer: "Because the two bags of tapioca are worth one (bag) of peanuts."

Transformations.   In this case, the children described or compared the elements in the proposed transformations. For example, to justify her answer to the verbal problem on Renata and Claudia's printed cards (Item 16), child #99 explained that they still had the same number of cards because they got the same number of cards from their aunt.

Logical Justifications.   Here the children mentioned that the amounts being compared were equal at the beginning and that the transformations were equal (or different) to justify that the equality would be (or would not be) maintained. In most of the cases, logical justifications referred to the specific situation and objects being dealt with, as in the following example from child #45 on Item 16 of the quantities task: "We will have the same because the two yellow boxes had the same as the orange box and then, if you add one red box and you add one red box we will have the same quantity." In other cases they were of a general nature as when, to justify her answers to Item 4 in the quantities task, child #24 explained: "It will be the same because we had the same and we are adding the same amount, then it will continue being the same."

Table 2.3 shows the total number of justifications of each type for all the items in the four contexts.

The computation and final state justifications focus on the amounts to remain should the proposed changes be implemented. These were slightly less frequent than justifications referring to the proposed transformations (transformation and logical justifications), with 43.07% of the total number of justifications against 49.27%.

Even though the percentage of logical answers was relatively low (13.28%), nearly every child provided a logical justification at least once, expressing it either in general terms or in relation to the specific amounts being dealt with. Only 12 children (four 7-year-olds, four 8-year-olds, two 9-year-olds, and two 10-year-olds) failed to ever give a complete, logical justification.

Figure 2.3 shows the number of children in each age group who gave at least one logical justification for tasks in each of the four contexts.

Age and Context Effects on Children's Justifications

Let's now look at how the different types of justifications produced by the children related to their age across the four task contexts. In each case, we used the Analysis of Variance (ANOVA) and Fisher PLSD specific com-

TABLE 2.3
Frequency and Percentage of Each Type of Justification for All Tasks

	Unclear	Computation	Final State	Transformation	Logical	Total
Total	294	681	973	1382	510	3840
Percent	7.66	17.73	25.34	35.99	13.28	100.00

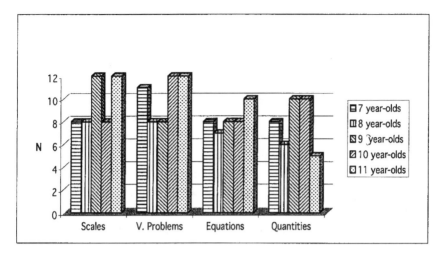

FIG. 2.3.   Number of children in each age group who gave at least one logical justification in each context.

parisons test to determine the significance of effects and of specific observed differences.

Unclear Justifications.   These were rare (see Fig. 2.4) across all contexts and significantly decreased with age ($F_{4,220} = 10.424, p < .0001$). The mean number of these answers was significantly higher among 7-year-olds in comparison to 8- ($p = .0045$), 9- ($p < .0001$), 10- ($p < .0001$), and

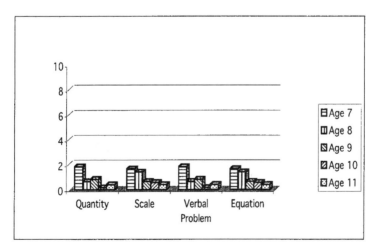

FIG. 2.4.   Mean number of unclear justifications.

11- ($p < .0001$) year-olds; and among 8-year-olds in comparison to 10- ($p = .0074$), and 11- ($p = .0120$) year-olds.

Computational Justifications. The mean number of computational justifications (see Fig. 2.5) was significantly affected by context ($F_{3,220} = 9.647, p < .0001$) and by age ($F_{4,220} = 4.037, p < .005$). Equation contexts were more likely to elicit computational justifications than scale ($p = .0002$), quantity ($p < .0001$), and verbal problem ($p < .0001$) contexts. Additionally, younger children were less likely to rely on computational justifications than the older children. The mean number of computational justifications was significantly larger in the equation context in comparison to the scale ($p = .0002$), quantity ($p < .0001$), and verbal problem contexts ($p < .0001$) and significantly smaller for 7-year-olds in comparison to 8- ($p = .0007$), 9- ($p = .0366$), 10- ($p = .0006$), and 11- ($p = .0107$) year-olds. No significant interaction effects were found.

Final State Justifications. Verbal problems were less likely to elicit final state justifications and 7-year-olds were more likely to rely on final state justifications than older children (see Fig. 2.6). We found significant effects due to context ($F_{3,220} = 50.437, p < .0001$), age ($F_{4,220} = 2.478, p = .0451$), and the interaction between context and age ($F_{12,220} = 1.978, p = .0274$) on the mean number of final state justifications. The mean num-

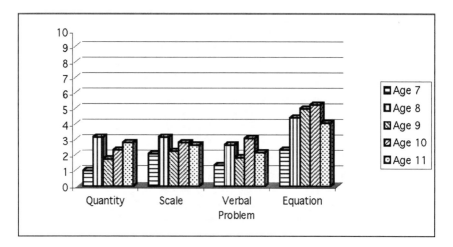

FIG. 2.5. Mean number of computational justifications.

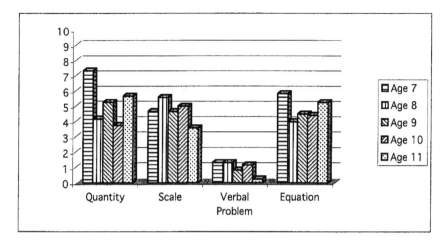

FIG. 2.6.   Mean number of final state justifications.

ber of this type of justification was significantly lower for verbal problems in comparison to the scale ($p < .0001$), quantity ($p < .0001$), and equation contexts ($p < .0001$), and significantly higher for 7-year-olds in comparison to 8-year-olds ($p = .213$), 9-year-olds ($p = .0272$), 10-year-olds ($p = .0066$), and 11-year-olds ($p = .0129$).

Transformational Justifications.   Verbal problems and the quantity context elicited transformation justifications more frequently than did the scale or the equation tasks (see Fig. 2.7). Transformational justifications were significantly affected by context ($F_{3,220} = 26.262, p < .0001$), with no age or interaction effects. The mean number of transformational justifications was significantly larger in the verbal problems in comparison to the scale ($p < .0001$), quantity ($p < .0001$), and equation contexts ($p < .0001$), and significantly larger in the quantity context, in comparison to the scale ($p = .0173$) and equation contexts ($p = .0066$).

Logical Justifications.   As expected, logical justifications (see Fig. 2.8) were significantly affected by age ($F_{4,220} = 3.961, p = .0040$). They were also significantly affected by context ($F_{3,220} = 9.039, p < .0001$), appearing more frequently in verbal problems than in the scale ($p = .0018$), quantity ($p < .0001$), or equation ($p < .0001$) contexts. The interaction between age and context was also significant ($F_{12,220} = 2.206, p < .0001$): children in the old-

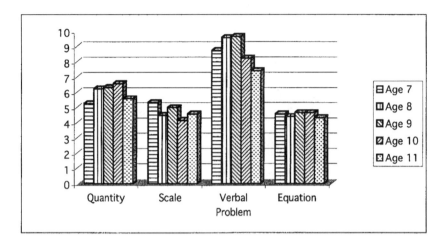

FIG. 2.7.   Mean number of transformational justifications.

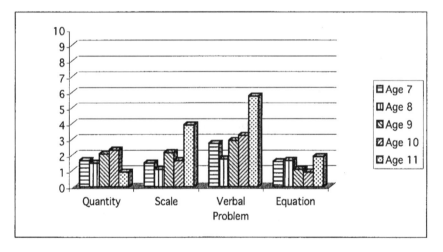

FIG. 2.8.   Mean number of logical justifications.

est age group (11-year-olds) produced a significantly higher mean number of logical justifications in comparison to 7- ($p = .0040$), 8- ($p = .0002$), 9- ($p = .0142$), and 10- ($p = .0124$) year-old children in the scale, verbal problem, and equation contexts, but not in the quantities context.

Our next question and final step in the analysis of the Brazilian children interview data focused on how the presence or absence of numerical information would relate to the children's justifications.

Effects Due to Numerical Information

Figures 2.9, 2.10, 2.11, and 2.12 show, for each context, the percentage of justifications of each type when all values were known (All), when only partial values were known (Partial), and when none of the values were known (None).

Across all contexts, when all the resulting values were known, children tended to carry out computations. In the quantity and verbal tasks, transformation answers were also very frequent when all values were known. Transformational and logical justifications were more likely to appear when

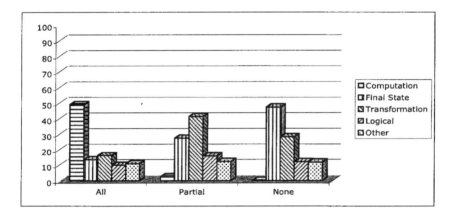

FIG. 2.9. Percent of each type of justification by knowledge of values in the scale task.

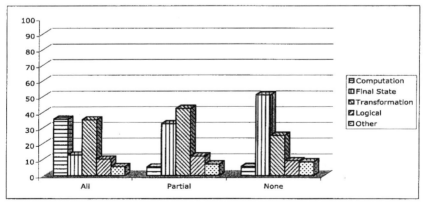

FIG. 2.10. Percent of each type of justification by knowledge of values in the quantity task.

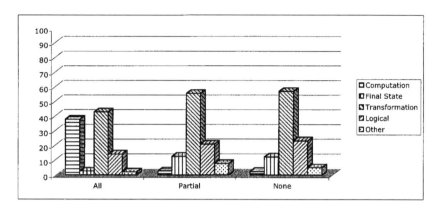

FIG. 2.11.   Percent of each type of justification by knowledge of values
in the verbal problem task.

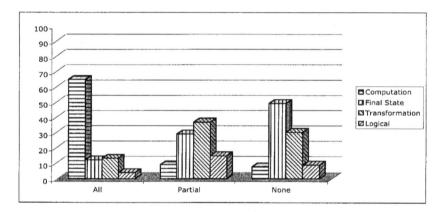

FIG. 2.12.   Percent of each type of justification by knowledge of values
in the equation task.

values were not known or were only partially known. In these cases, we also
found a high frequency of final state justifications in the scale, quantity, and
equations tasks.

DISCUSSION

Even 7-year-olds understand one of the basic principles of algebra, namely,
that if equals are added or subtracted to equals, the equation still holds. Use
of this principle, however, depends on the ways problems are presented.

Verbal problems elicited more logical and transformational justifications than problems with concrete counters, objects on a scale, or equations. Computational justifications or justifications that focused on the final result of transformations were more often elicited by problems with concrete counters, objects on a scale, or equations. Items where all numerical values were known overwhelmingly elicited computation answers whereas those where the values to remain in the comparison were unknown or partially known more often elicited other types of justifications.

Although children often seemed to search for arithmetical solutions, attributing values to the unknowns, most students showed at least once that they were able to solve the problems taking into account basic algebraic principles. School training on the solution of arithmetic problems may have created the strictly computational approach to solve problems involving numbers that prevents children from more often focusing on the logical aspects of mathematics.

These preliminary findings are rather encouraging. If even 7-year-olds can understand some basic logical principles related to algebra, it may be possible to introduce algebraic activities in the mathematics curriculum much earlier than is usually the case. Our findings also suggest that verbal problems, more than equations and concrete models such as counters or a balance scale, constitute a better context to elicit children's logical justifications. The same is true for the partially known amounts as opposed to problems where all the amounts involved are either known or completely unknown.

In the study with Brazilian children, we did not explore how far children would use their basic understanding about the preservation of equalities to solve algebraic problems. This is the focus of our analysis in chapter 3. There, we first report on a partial replication of the study with Brazilian children with a group of U.S. third-graders. In the second part of the chapter, we analyze how some of these same children attempt to solve algebraic problems using intuitive notations and their understanding about when equalities are preserved.

3

Can Young Students Solve Equations?[4]

Analúcia D. Schliemann
David W. Carraher
Bárbara M. Brizuela
Wendy Jones

We saw in chapter 2 that even 7-year-old children acknowledge that equal amounts remain equal when another amount is added to or taken away from each. The amounts change, but the condition of being equal continues to hold true. Moreover, under certain circumstances, children provide logical justifications for their answers. This finding suggests that children may be able to begin dealing with algebraic relations at a young age. But can they actually solve algebraic problems for unknown values? And can they use notation to do so?

We suspect that if children can express general algebraic properties and relations through natural language, they also can express these properties and relations in written form. But, ultimately, we will have to defer to the results of research. This chapter aims to move us closer to this goal.

In the two studies we describe in this chapter, we extend the analysis we begun in chapter 2. Here we attempt to replicate, among U.S. children, our previous findings. In a follow-up study, we examine how the same children handle two algebra problems.

---

[4]An earlier version of this work was presented at the EARG II (the second meeting of the Early Algebra Research Group, University of Massachusetts at Dartmouth/Tufts University, 1998).

STUDY 1: RECOGNIZING INVARIANCE DESPITE
CHANGE: STRATEGIES AND REPRESENTATIONS

In this interview study, we examined how a group of U.S. third graders approach part of the verbal problems included in the study with Brazilian children (chap. 2). We looked at how, in the context of verbal problems, they understand that if we add or subtract equal amounts from each side of a given equality, the equality holds and that, if the amounts to be added or subtracted are different, the equality ceases to hold. We also examined, in depth, one child's written notations to represent the problems she was asked to solve.

Method

Nineteen 3rd graders from the same classroom of a public school in a Boston suburb were individually interviewed and asked to solve eight verbal problems. For each problem, the interviewer read or asked the child to read a short story where two people were described as having, initially, the same number of objects. Then, equal or different quantities of objects were added or taken away from the previous equivalent amounts. The child was asked to determine whether the two people in the story still had the same amount of objects. The eight problems presented to this group of children are shown in Table 3.1.

We have represented the structure of the problems through equations in Table 3.1. This is merely for our convenience; the children were shown only the word problems, not the equations. We used numbers to express amounts in Equations 1 to 4 because Word Problems 1 to 4 provide numerical information for all the quantities. We used letters to represent unknown amounts in Equations 5 to 8 because Word Problems 5 to 8 do not specify numbers.

The question marks above each equals sign in Table 3.1 are meant to highlight the fact that the equation reflects an issue to be solved rather than a statement of fact; indeed as was the case in chapter 2, sometimes the equation holds, sometimes it does not. For Problems 1, 4, 5, and 7, the transformations on the two quantities (sides of the equation) were equivalent; for Problems 2, 3, 6, and 8, the transformations were not.

For each problem, children were allowed to use whatever tools and representations they judged necessary to reach a solution and were asked to justify their answers. Paper, pencil, and colored markers were available on

TABLE 3.1

Problems Used in Study 1

Word Problems Given	Implicit Equations (Not Shown to Children)
Problems With Specified Amounts	
1. Brian and Tim love to eat chocolate. One day, Brian took 10 chocolates to school and then bought 2 more at the school store. Tim brought 5 chocolates, then bought 5 more in the school store, and then got 2 more from another friend. During break time, Tim ate 2 of his chocolates and Brian also ate 2 of his chocolates. Now, do you think that after the break Tim has the same amount of chocolates as Brian? Or, do you think one has more chocolates than the other?	$10 + 2 = 5 + 5 + 2$ $10 + 2 (-2) = 5 + 5 + 2 (-2)$ [true]
2. Barbara and Joanna both had birthday parties on the same day. Barbara got 7 presents from her friends, and Joanna also got 7 presents from her friends. When each party was over, both girls had a special family time and they received more presents. Barbara received 6 more presents from her family. Joanna received 3 more presents from her family. At the end of the day, do you think that Joanna has the same amount of gifts as Barbara? Or, do you think that one has more gifts than the other?	$7 = 7$ $7 (+ 6) = 7 (+ 3)$ [false]
3. Patricia and Daniel are neighbors playing outside. They both like oranges, so each went back to their house to get oranges. Patricia brought out 6 oranges and Daniel brought out 3. Each ran back to their house to get more oranges. Patricia brought out 4 more oranges and Daniel brought out 3 more oranges. Daniel ran back a third time and returned with 4 more oranges. At this time, a friend came over. Patricia gave 6 oranges to their friend, and Daniel gave 3 oranges. Now, do you think after they shared that Patricia and Daniel had the same amount of oranges? Or, do you think that one has more oranges than the other?	$6 + 4 = 3 + 3 + 4$ $6 + 4 (-6) = 3 + 3 + 4 (- 3)$ [false]

(continued)

TABLE 3.1

(continued)

Word Problems Given	Implicit Equations (Not Shown to Children)
Problems With Specified Amounts	
4. Bobby and Sara are playing with marbles. Bobby takes 4 marbles out of his left pocket and puts them on the ground. Bobby then takes 4 more marbles out of his right pocket and places them on the ground. Sara carries 8 marbles from the container and places them on the ground. After that Sara finds 2 marbles and places them on the ground. Bobby also finds 2 marbles and places them on the ground. Do you think that Bobby has the same amount of marbles as Sara? Or do you think that one has more marbles than the other?	$4 + 4 = 8$ $4 + 4 (+2) = 8 (+2)$ [true]
Problems With Unspecified Amounts	
5. Bob and Andrew were collecting sea shells on the beach early in the morning. Bob put the shells he found in a big box. Andrew found the same number of shells as Bob did, but put them evenly in two small boxes. In the afternoon, they went back to the beach and Bob again found the same amount of shells as Andrew did. This time each boy put the shells they had found in a bag. The next day they went to count how many shells each one had but they could not find the bags. Do you think that Bob has the same number of shells as Andrew does? Or do you think that one of them has more shells than the other?	$x = y + y$ $x + z (-z) = y + y + z (-z)$ [true]
6. Charlie and Renée love cookies. They each had a batch of cookies of the same amount. Charlie put all of his cookies into one basket. Renée put her cookies evenly into two baskets. Then, another batch came out of the oven. Charlie and Renée took the same amount of cookies, but this time they both put the new cookies in a bag to keep fresh to eat later. Charlie's little sister came into the kitchen where they were and said that she wanted some cookies too. Charlie gave her his basket of cookies and Renée gave her one of her baskets of cookies. Now, do you think that after they shared their cookies that Charlie had the same number of cookies as Renée? Or do you think that one had more cookies than the other?	$x + z = y + y + z$ $x + z (-x) = y + y + z + (-y)$ [false]

(continued)

TABLE 3.1
(continued)

Word Problems Given	Implicit Equations (Not Shown to Children)
Problems With Unspecified Amounts	
7. Rose and Claudia collected stamps. Before Christmas, Rose had the same number of stamps as Claudia did. Rose had all her stamps in 1 stamp book. Claudia kept her stamps in 2 stamp books. After Christmas, they collected all the stamps from Christmas cards their families received and realized that they had each received the same number of new stamps and went to file them in their books. Do you think that now Rose has the same number of stamps as Claudia? Or do you think that one of them has more stamps than the other?	$x = y1 + y2$ $x (+ z) = y1 + y2 (+ z)$ [true]
8. One weekend, Mike and Rob went fishing at the pier. On Saturday they both caught the same number of fish. Mike and Rob went back to the pier on Sunday. At the end of the day, they counted how many fish each had in their buckets. They discovered that, on this day, Mike caught more fish than Rob. At the end of the weekend, do you think that Mike had caught the same amount of fish as Rob? Or do you think that one caught more fish than the other?	$x = x$ $y > z$ $x + y = x + z$ [false]

the table for children to use during problem solving or during the justification phase.

Results

Children responded correctly in the great majority of cases (135 of 143 responses, or 94.4%), recognizing that equal operations on equal quantities yield equal results and that unequal operations to equal quantities yield unequal results. Children used two main strategies to work out an answer or to justify their answers (see Table 3.2).

In the first strategy, computation of values, the children started from the initial amounts and then added or subtracted the amounts mentioned in the

TABLE 3.2
Number of Problems by Type and Solution Strategy

Problem Type	Solution Strategies		
	Computation	Logical	Other
Numerical amounts specified (Problems 1–4)	44 (57.9%)	24 (31.6%)	8 (10.5%)
Unspecified amounts (Problems 5–8)	3 (4.0%)	60 (79.0%)	13 (17.0%)

transformations for each one of the characters in the problem, comparing the results thus obtained at the end. This was children's preferred (57.9%) strategy for problems containing numerical information. In the second strategy, children focused on the transformations that took place in the story, stressing whether they were the same or different. Most of the children choosing this approach emphasized the logical necessity of their conclusions stating that, if the transformations were the same (or different), then the final quantities should be the same (or different). As many as 79.0% of the responses to the problems with no specified amounts were of this type.

The two different types of problems also elicited different representations. The following excerpt from the interview with Eliza provides some insight into how children approached the two types of problems; her interview also highlights the role that notations played in her approach to these problems.

To solve Problems 1, 2, and 3, Eliza displayed the numerical information in two columns. She first wrote the children's names and, under each name, the respective numerical information and the resulting quantities. After solving Problem 3, performing the written computations shown in Fig. 3.1, Eliza explained, "I wrote the numbers to remember what to minus and what to add."

When asked if she could solve the next problem (Problem 4) without pencil and paper, she put them aside and started reading the problem.[5] But after reading a few lines she gave up and said that she needed pencil and

---

[5]The motivation for this request was that the interviewer wanted to assess what role the representations themselves might have on Eliza's solution process for the problems.

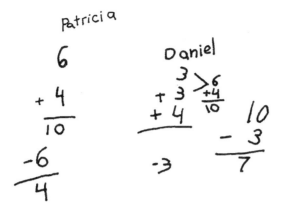

FIG. 3.1. Eliza's notation to solve Problem 3.

paper. The interviewer read the problem and Eliza again listed the numerical information in two columns, one for each person in the problem (see Fig. 3.2).

Eliza started working on the computations and mistakenly concluded that, at the end, Sara had 10 and Bobby had 6 marbles. She then read the story once more and, realizing her mistake, concluded that they had equal amounts. She explained that she had thought that one of the signs that she had written was a minus sign instead of a plus sign. She justified her final answer exclusively on the basis of the arithmetical computations performed: "Both have 10 marbles at the end 'cause 8 plus 2 makes 10."

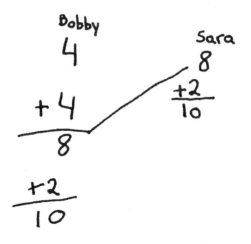

FIG. 3.2. Eliza's notation to solve Problem 4.

This passage shows that the written notation serves more than to *register* her thinking; it also has a directive role *guiding* her thinking. When she incorrectly read a plus sign as a minus sign, she carried out a subtraction and obtained a wrong answer. It is also significant that the presence of numbers in the problem evoked a computational response in Eliza. She was trying not to take notes, but gave up and started writing the numbers in the problem, computing the results.

Throughout the children's solutions to the problems with numerical information, the notations facilitated finding an answer. In Figs. 3.1 and 3.2, we see how Eliza wrote out all of the actions that were described in the word problem, including the substeps in the problem and didn't take them for granted. At times, she used the notations to remind herself of what had happened in the story. For example, in Fig. 3.1 Eliza wrote "−3" at the bottom. She did not incorporate this notation into any specific computation, but seemed to have written it in order to keep track of the events that took place in the problem. She represents the different actions that take place in the story, and then she also carries out other actions through the computations that she represents and performs. She seems comfortable enough with the notations so that she can allow herself to play around with them. In both Figs. 3.1 and 3.2, she combines the computations in interesting ways, through the drawing of lines and brackets.

What does she do when no numerical information is provided? As the interviewer read Problem 5, Eliza wrote the names of the characters in the story and seemed to be waiting for more information. After a while, as it became evident that no precise numerical information would be provided, she placed the pencil aside and, pausing briefly after the problem was read, concluded that Bob and Andrew had the same number of shells and provided a logical explanation for her conclusion:

> **Eliza:** It didn't tell you how many they had *so I didn't have to do any math* but in the beginning it said that the boxes were equal; but it said that the bags were equal too so if both bags were gone and the boxes are equal then they'd have the same number of shells. (Emphasis added.)

Eliza solved this problem mentally by analyzing the relationships between the different amounts. Instead of performing computations, she compared the equal initial state in the amount of shells each boy had, then compared the transformations, which were also equal, and concluded that this led to an equal final state.

The interviewer (Bárbara) asked Eliza to clarify what "doing math" involves:

Bárbara: And what did you mean when you said that you "didn't have to do any math?"

Eliza: Well, it didn't really tell you how many they had, but it told you that the bags weren't there, and earlier it said that they had the same amount for the boxes.

Bárbara: Um . . .

Eliza: So. I thought that . . . if the same number was for the bags and the same number was for the boxes, that if the bags weren't there then the boxes will still be even.

Eliza consulted the problem again:

Eliza: See, I just had to read over part of it to see . . .

Bárbara: So, math . . . you mean that you just do math when there are numbers there?

Eliza: (Pause.) Yeah.

Bárbara: And do you prefer there to be numbers, or not, or is it the same?

Eliza: Um, pretty much the same.

Bárbara: [Pointing to notations for Problem 5.] And is that why you didn't write anything for that?

Eliza: Yeah, cause I thought there would be numbers [in the problem], because usually I don't skim through it [the problem] before I read it because then I'll just have to go back again.

Eliza espouses a view of mathematics as involving numbers and computations as opposed to logical relations. Her view may well reflect traditional curricula focus. Moreover, in her case, notations are necessary only when there are computations to be carried out.

The interviewer then read Problem 6 aloud. In Fig. 3.3, we see how Eliza sought to represent a problem that offered no numerical information that could be used in computations. Eliza started out wanting to write the parts and different steps in the story, as she had done in Figs. 3.1 and 3.2

for Problems 3 and 4. She wanted to keep track of the numerical information and then do something with those numbers.

As she continued listening to the problem, she found that there was really nothing to be done with the numbers that she had represented. In Fig. 3.3, we see how Eliza tried to use abbreviations to represent "batch" and "basket," but then found herself in trouble because both words start with the same letter. We might hypothesize that the *b* Eliza wrote is her own version of an *x* in a problem dealing with variable quantities. After a while, Eliza stated that Charlie and Renée had the same amount of cookies and explained:

> **Eliza:** In the beginning each had a batch of cookies, Charlie put it in one basket and Renée put it in 2 but they were the same number of cookies. Charlie gave all of his basket but he still had half of the other batch and she still has half a batch. No . . . [pause] she has more than him cause she still has the other half of the batch.

The interviewer asked her why she wrote what she wrote and she answers:

> **Eliza:** I thought it would be harder than just figuring it out in my head if I tried it on paper cause there aren't too many numbers and it's harder to do on paper and it's easier to do in your head.

Eliza used notations to help her go through the process of solving a problem when there is numerical information in it. For problems with no numerical information, it was easier for her to solve the problems "in [her] head." We might wonder what might happen, however, with children who have more difficulties than Eliza does with solving problems "in [her] head."

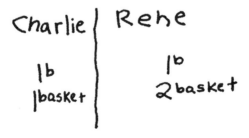

FIG. 3.3.   Eliza's notation to solve Problem 6.

How would they go about solving the problem? Would they spontaneously look for ways of representing? Or might representations be helpful to them in trying to solve the problems? We dealt with these questions in the study described next, when we asked children to determine the values of unknown amounts in verbal problems.

STUDY 2: "BUT HOW MUCH, HOW MANY?": THE PARADOX INHERENT IN REPRESENTING UNKNOWN QUANTITIES

The issue before children in Study 1 was to determine whether two quantities remained equal after equal or unequal additive transformations were carried out on both sides of an equation. When numbers were salient, they tended to carry out computations and compare the results. One might wrongly surmise from their approach that they did not appreciate the logic of equal operations to equal things. However, in the condition where numbers were not salient they appealed to this general principle. This suggests that the children may be able to solve equations.

Study 2 challenged the same children to use such knowledge in order to determine the values of unknown quantities in verbal problems. This amounted to asking children to solve equations, even though they were unfamiliar with algebraic notation and algebraic rules for operating on equations. Bodanskii's (1991) study showed that elementary school children can adopt and make use of a well-structured notation system for solving algebra problems. However, his study left unanswered many questions concerning children's understanding of algebra, especially in what concerns their spontaneous use of notations and algebraic procedures to solve equations.

In this case, we chose to focus on two linear equations that were also part of a study by Brito Lima (1996; see also Brito Lima & da Rocha Falcão, 1997). The first one can be represented by the equation $8 + x = 3x$. The second involves two variables and can be represented by $7 + y = 2 + y + x$. For each equation, canceling one unknown on each side of the equation greatly simplifies the search for a solution. But how would children proceed? What kind of notation would they spontaneously use? Do children need support in developing a notation? If so, what kind of help is needed for this notation to be developed by the child? And, once a written representation is achieved, how do they proceed to compute a result? Would they use the canceling-out strategy or some other method? These were the questions that guided our analysis of the interviews conducted with third graders while they tried to solve the two equations. It is important to emphasize that the equations were given as word problems; no equations were shown to children. We were nonetheless interested in observing the notations they would produce, spontaneously or with encouragement from the interviewer, to clarify and support their thinking. The way in which they understood and made use of notations, even if they departed from conventions for representing equations, could inform us about how they approached the problems put before them.

Method

After solving the problems in Study 1, some of the children were also asked to individually solve six new problems, in the sequence shown in Table 3.3. As before, the interviewer verbally presented or asked each child to read each problem and try to solve it. The interview was conducted in a flexible way, with questions and prompts that might help the child to find a path towards a solution. Children were allowed to use whatever tools and representations they judged necessary to reach a solution and were asked to justify their answers.

Problems 1 to 4, where unknown amounts appeared on only one side of the equation, served as warm-up tasks; the two target problems of our analysis were Problems 5 and 6. Not all the problems were given to all children because some of them showed that they were tired or not interested in pursuing the interview. As a result, six children were given both Problem 5 and 6, nine were given Problem 5 only, and four were given Problem 6 only. The analysis that follows refers therefore to the responses of 15 children to Problem 5 (the "fish problem") and of 10 children to Problem 6 (the "apples problem").

Results

In terms of children's general solution strategies, of the 15 children who were given the "fish problem," two were able to independently find a solution, nine found a solution after receiving prompts from the examiner, and

TABLE 3.3

Problems Used in Study 2

Problems Given	Problem Structure (Not Shown to Children)
Warm-up Problems [Unknown Quantities on One Side Only]	
1. Suzie and Liz spent the day selling Girl Scout cookies. Suzie sold 4 boxes of cookies in the morning and a few more boxes in the afternoon. Liz sold 7 boxes during the whole day. When they met at the end of the day they realized that they had sold the same number of boxes. How many boxes did Suzie sell in the afternoon?	$4 + x = 7$ $x = ?$
2. David and Jenny played marbles today. At the end of the game, David had one pile of green marbles, and Jenny also had one pile of green marbles. Both piles had the same number of marbles. They counted up all the marbles and found that there were 10. How many marbles were in each pile?	$x + x = 10$ $x = ?$
3. Sara and Jimmy went to the garden to pick some flowers. Jimmy picked 1 bunch of red flowers. Sara picked 2 bunches of red flowers. Each bunch has the same number of red flowers. When they added up all the flowers, they discovered that there were 12 flowers in all. How many flowers were in each bunch?	$3x = 12$ $x = ?$
4. Mary and Joe went to different homes on Halloween. In the first house Mary received a bag of purple candies. In the second house, she received three times as many purple candies as in the first house. She then met Joe who had, overall, received 20 purple candies. Mary then counted her candies and realized that she had the same number of purple candies as Joe. How many purple candies did Mary receive in the first house?	$x + 3x = 20$ $x = ?$
Target Problems [Unknown Quantities on Both Sides]	
5. Mike and Rob each had a water tank with fish. Mike has 8 blue fish and some red fish. Rob only has red fish; he has three times as many red fish as Mike. Overall, Mike has the same number of fish as Rob. How many red fish does Mike have?	$8 + x = 3x$ $x = ?$
6. Jessica and Kelly went apple picking so that they could make some pies. Jessica picked 7 red apples and a few green apples. Kelly picked 2 red apples, the same number of green apples as did Jessica, and a few yellow apples. At the end Jessica had the same number of apples as did Kelly. How many yellow apples did Kelly pick?	$7 + y = 2 + y + x$ $x = ?$

four children couldn't solve the problem even when help was provided. The two children who independently found a solution wrote the number "8" on paper and then proceeded to mentally solve the problem, refusing the examiner's suggestions to represent the unknown amounts in writing. When asked to explain further, one of them answered that four "would be the only logical answer." Two of the four children who did not find a solution stated that they needed to know "how many is a few?" and that the problem had no solution. The other two initiated a process of developing a written representation for the problem but appeared distracted and, although receiving help from the examiner, could not find a solution.

The initial difficulties showed by the nine children who solved the fish problem with help were related to dealing with the unknown quantities. Some appeared puzzled and commented that "We don't know," or that "We don't have the number." Others stated or guessed that "a few," or "some" should mean two or three. The help provided to these children initially consisted of suggestions to represent unknown quantities as some shape. Once a representation was achieved, most children would come up with a guess (usually three) for how many "a few red fish" would be. Such reaction shows that the use of a notation for an unknown quantity left unaffected their idea that a few should be two or three. The interviewer would then suggest that they could test their guess and, when the guess led to an inequality, children were encouraged to try other numbers until an equality between the two sides of the equation was found.

Of the 10 children attempting to solve the "apples problem," five found a solution without any help, three solved the problem after receiving help, and two were not able to find an answer. Two of the children who solved the apples problem without help started by attributing a value of three to "a few green apples." Starting with this value, one of them immediately stated that five was the value that would lead to equal amounts while the other tried different values until one that would maintain the equality was found. Two other children immediately gave a correct answer and the fifth child (Charles, see the following detailed description) gave the correct answer after spontaneously drawing shapes to represent unknown amounts of apples, an approach he developed with the interviewer's help while trying to solve the "fish problem." The two children who tried but were not able to find a solution also started by attributing a value to "a few green ap-

ples," but were lost in the computations involved in finding out the number of yellow apples.

The apples problem entailed unknown amounts appearing on both sides of an equation. Such unknown amounts—the number of green apples—could be canceled out or assume any value without destroying the equality. We analyzed how children dealt with them while working out a solution and how they answered the interviewer's question about whether any number of green apples would maintain the equality. Two children spontaneously showed a clear understanding that any value could be attributed to the green apples. Two other children, as some of the children in Brito Lima's (1996) study, showed an implicit understanding that the number of green apples didn't matter but, once asked to state whether that was true, went through a few tests of different values before explicitly stating that any value would do. Although they apparently understood that the equal amounts could assume any values without altering the equality, when directly asked to state whether the number of green apples matters, they needed to test different numbers, treating the conclusion as a matter of induction instead of a necessary logical deduction.

The following descriptions of how individual children proceeded exemplify children's typical approaches to the two problems. As the interviewer read the problem, one of the children (Maggie, see Fig. 3.4) took notes, organizing them along two columns. When asked to represent the quantities, she represented eight fish as eight tallies, "a few fish" by a drawing of one fish, and "three times as many fish" as a fish with three

FIG. 3.4.   Maggie's notation to solve the "fish problem."

lines above it. She then guessed that Mike would have three red fish. On the interviewer's suggestion to check whether this would lead to equal amounts, she added $8 + 3$ and compared the result to 3×3, stating that 3 was not the right answer. She then tried 5 and, finally, 4 concluding that 4 was the right answer. Maggie used her representation to organize the information presented in the problem and to organize her thoughts and solution process for the problem.

Some children immediately integrated the suggestions to represent the known and unknown quantities in interesting ways, as in Melanie's case, who represented "a few red fish" as a bucket of fish and "three times as many red fish" as three buckets. Two children spontaneously showed a clear understanding that the amounts of green apples for each girl in the problem did not matter because they were the same. This is clearly exemplified by the following dialogue with Melanie.

While the interviewer (Wendy) read the problem, Melanie wrote the initials of the characters and the number of red apples each had. Without any further notation, she promptly provided the correct answer:

Melanie: Five.

Wendy: And how did you get 5?

Melanie: Because 5 plus 2 equals 7.

Wendy: OK, but what about the green apples?

Melanie: She picked the same amount.

Wendy: Yes.

Melanie: Kelly picked the same amount *so it doesn't matter.*

Wendy: Why wouldn't it matter?

Melanie: Because they first have, they have to start off with the same amount so they end with the same amount.

We see here how Melanie, to compute the number of yellow apples, spontaneously eliminated the green apples, as one would do while solving a written equation.

Later, the interviewer asked Melanie to develop a representation for the unknown quantities, and to elaborate on the possible values for the green apples. She represented each unknown amount of green and yellow apples

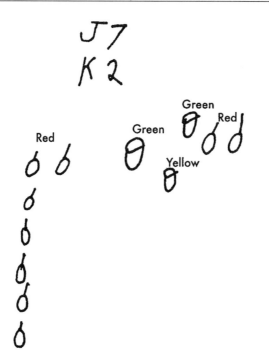

FIG. 3.5. Melanie's notation for the "apples problem."

through the drawing of a bucket (see Fig. 3.5), as she had done for the representation of "a few red fish" in the previous problem (not shown).
She then further explained:

Wendy: OK, great. Tell me how you did it.

Melanie: Five plus 2 equals 7.

Wendy: Yes.

Melanie: And since they both have one [bucket of green apples] . . . they have the same amount in the green bucket and at the end they have the same amount. So they get the, the umm, 5 plus 2 equals 7, and then they have the same amount in the green bucket, they have the same amount of greens, so they have, so she has 5 [yellow] apples.

Melanie's example is both similar and different to that of Eliza. Contrasting with Eliza's example, Melanie does not need to represent every single action or computation in her notation. However, like Eliza, Melanie had already solved the problem. The notation is just a *representation* of her thinking, of the solution that she has already arrived at. But, the question remains, what about children who have a harder time with mental math or logical relations problems?

In response to this question, other children needed more help, as the following transcript of Charles' interview illustrates. The interviewer (Wendy) started reading the "fish problem" to Charles:

Wendy: Mike and Joe each had a water tank with fish. Mike has 8 blue fish and some number of red fish.

Charles wrote down "8" and then looked at the interviewer as if puzzled by the expression "some number of red fish" and asked for help.

Wendy: We don't know. Rob only has red fish, but he has three times as many red fish as Mike.

Charles started to write something, but stopped and continued to listen.

Wendy: Now, overall, Mike and Rob have the same number of fish. How many red fish does Mike have?

Charles smiled and paused. He shook his head and said:

Charles: I don't know.

Sensing that developing some representation for the unknown quantity might prove helpful, the interviewer proceeded by asking some questions so that he could develop a written representation for the problem:

Wendy: How can you show 8 blue fish?
Charles: With an 8.
Wendy: OK, how can you show some number of red fish?
Charles: I don't know.

The interviewer suggested that he use the materials on the table to draw a figure to represent the red fish:

Wendy: OK, how about if we make a red shape on the paper?

Charles drew a red shape on the paper, next to the number "8," and colored it in (see Fig. 3.6).

Wendy: OK, now, what does that mean?
Charles: It's . . . [he shrugs his shoulders].
Wendy: It's some number, we don't know. It could be any number.

The interviewer then helped Charles represent "three times as many fish":

Wendy: [pointing to the red shape on the paper, shown on the left in Fig. 3.6]: How would you show three times that number of fish?
Charles: Three times 3 . . .
Wendy: How can you show three times this little red shape here [points to the shape on the paper]?
Charles: But we don't have . . . we don't have a number for this.
Wendy: Well, you're right, we don't have a number. How could we show three times as many red shapes?

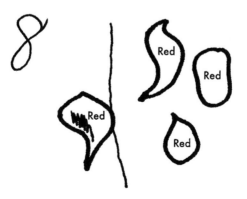

FIG. 3.6.   Charles' notation to solve the "fish problem."

Charles smiled nervously and the interviewer took another approach. She pointed and made a circle with her pen cap around Charles' notation (on the left in Fig. 3.6) and continued:

Wendy:	OK, this is Mike here, right? How about if you put Rob over here [motioning to physically separate the notations]?
Charles:	So he has red fish.
Wendy:	How many red fish?
Charles:	We don't know.
Wendy:	We don't know. Three times as many red fish as Mike.
Charles:	But we don't know ...
Wendy:	We don't know what the number is, but how could we draw it?
Charles:	With a red thing?
Wendy:	How many red things? Rob has three times this many [points to the red shape drawing representing the few fish Mike has, on the left in Fig. 3.6]. So, what could we draw for Rob?
Charles:	But, we don't know how many fish this is.

Given Charles's insistence that we did not know how many red fish Rob has because we do not have a number, the interviewer took a more direct approach:

Wendy:	You're right, how about if we draw three of these [points to the red shape, on the left of Fig. 3.6]?

Charles drew the three red shapes to represent Rob's fish. Once a written representation for all the elements in the problem was achieved, the interviewer continued:

Wendy:	Now, we know that Mike and Rob have the same number of fish altogether. So what can you tell me about this? Let's put a line here [the interviewer draws a line between the two sets of drawings].
Charles:	It would have to be ... Are those [the two sides of the drawing] the same amount of fish?
Wendy:	Yes, those are the same amount of fish on each side.

Charles paused for a moment and said, while examining his notations:

Charles: It would have to be . . . three fish here . . . oh . . .

Wendy: Let's start with that. If there is three fish here [pointing to the shape representing Mike's red fish], how many fish does Mike have?

Charles: So far we know that he has eight?

Wendy: And, if this is three fish like you said [pointing to the circle in Mike's side], how many does he have?

Charles: Eleven.

Wendy: OK. Now, we know that Mike and Rob have the same number of fish, right? If you put three fish in each of these little circles, how many does he have?

Instead of following the interviewer's suggestion to try out number three, Charles paused for a while and then answered:

Charles: So that would be 4 for each one. There are 4 in each one.

Wendy: Are there 4 in here [pointing to the shape for Mike's red fish] too?

Charles: Yeah, there would have to be. Twelve. Twelve and twelve.

The dialogue just reviewed may suggest that the interviewer was providing too much help and that Charles was simply executing step-by-step orders, without fully understanding the problem. The "fish problem" was clearly very difficult for him, as he was convinced that he couldn't represent or operate on unknown quantities. When assisted in developing and using the notation, he still had difficulties in understanding what was going on. Towards the end, though, aware that the two sides of his representation needed to be the same, he was able to consider different values for the unknown quantities, thus finding a value satisfying the equation.

As we will see next, his prompt reaction to the "apple problem" suggests that in the "fish problem" he was, in fact, learning how to use notations to solve problems. After the interviewer read the problem, Charles immediately produced the drawing in Fig. 3.7 and promptly presented the right answer.

Unlike Maggie and Melanie, who did not use their notations to solve the problem, but to represent a solution they arrived at mentally, Charles seemed to begin to integrate his prior strategies of trial and er-

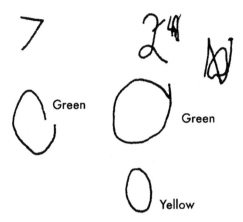

FIG. 3.7. Charles' notation for the "apples problem."

ror and guessing with the use of notations as a meaning for reaching a solution.

Results of this second study highlight two difficulties children must overcome to solve algebra problems. The first one consists of developing a notation for the unknown quantities. None of the children spontaneously used shapes to represent the unknown quantities while solving the "fish problem" and only one did so when solving the "apple problem." The second difficulty consists in accepting to work out a solution from unknown quantities. Children's comments stating that more information was needed to solve the problems and their frequent attempts to attribute specific values to "a few" suggest that the difficulty they encounter may result from their experiences with arithmetical problems at school, where solutions to problems are always found through operations on known quantities.

Once these problems are overcome, spontaneously or after suggestions from the interviewer, they can work out a solution by trying out different values until one that satisfies the equation is found. As found in studies with adolescents (see Chazan, 1993; Fishbein & Keden, 1982; Lee & Wheeler, 1989; and Morris, 1995), students require empirical testing. This type of solution strategy, although still an arithmetic solution, may constitute a first step towards the development of children's understanding of equations and of algebraic procedures to solve them. Because they understand that equal transformations on the two sides of an equality do not destroy the equality, children may be able to later develop an algebraic solution to the equation representing the relationships in the problem. Also, children's understanding that equal unknown quantities on the two sides of an equality can assume any value without destroying the equality might constitute a step towards the understanding and representation of variables and functions.

GENERAL CONCLUSIONS

Taken together, these examples suggest that third graders can develop consistent notations to represent the elements and the relationships in problems involving known and unknown quantities. In this process, their use of circles and shapes to represent collective bunches may constitute a meaningful transitional notation between measured and unknown quantities. They can also use a canceling-out strategy to mentally eliminate equal amounts that appear on both sides of the equality they are dealing with. This suggests that they could learn the syntactic rules of algebra for dealing with unknown quantities that appear on both sides of equations. It also suggests that high school students' difficulties with unknowns that appear on both sides of the equation are not due to cognitive development, as was proposed by Filloy and Rojano (1989).

We did not explore how the children's intuitive notations would relate to more conventional representational systems. This is one of the goals of the classroom studies we report in the following chapters in Part II, as we explore other aspects of algebraic understanding among third-grade children in the classroom.

The examples presented in this chapter highlight at least three functions that notations come to hold for children:

- To represent all the actions and computations required to solve a problem. Eliza, in Study 1, provides an illustration of this function. This approach, of course, brings up conflicts for problems that contain no numerical information, but only express the logical relationships among quantities, be they unknown quantities or variables.

- To express relationships between unknown quantities, as Melanie and Maggie did in Study 2.
- To be able to actually solve the problem, as Charles did in Study 2.

These three functions should not be thought of as isolated or independent. There could, in fact, be overlaps between them. In fact, a question imposes itself about whether it is potentially necessary for children to develop notations that cover each one of these approaches in order to be able to solve algebraic problems.

Children's achievements in the individual interview situations described in this and in the previous chapter were very promising but cannot tell us about what they can do in the classroom. Researchers and practitioners know very well that lab research does not easily translate into classroom activities. As we planned for new studies on early algebra, it was clear to us that if we were to contribute to mathematics education our research had to move into the classroom. And that is what we did next. At the same time we changed our focus from equalities to the analysis of children's understanding of functions and variables. As we look at children's participation in algebraic activities in the classroom, we hope to further clarify issues related to the possibility of introducing algebra in the elementary school mathematics curriculum and to the choice of teaching activities that would allow for the full development of algebraic reasoning and procedures in elementary school.

Vygotsky's (1978) work has raised the intriguing prospect that representational tools, in mediating thought and communication, may actually transform cognition. One need not subscribe to the view that representational tools immediately and directly influence cognitive processes but, instead, one can conceive that tools channel and structure thought in ways that would not have otherwise occurred. Symbolic representations open up further avenues of thinking and evoke certain comparisons to things the learner already knows.

We believe that the tools and representational systems used by the individual play a role in the structure and direction of mathematical thinking, allowing for different aspects of mathematical reasoning to come to the forefront. We consider it necessary, thereby, to document how children's symbolic repertoire for expressing general algebraic properties gradually expands. From the perspective we take, children do not move suddenly from symbol-free expression to conventional written representations. Words are symbols. Diagrams are symbols. Written mathematical representation is symbolic whether or not it conforms to mathematical convention. The task before us is to document how children attempt to express, in writing, the relationships presented to them in verbal problems and how their written production may help them solve algebraic problems.

II

CLASSROOM STUDIES

Data from our interview studies were rather encouraging. We found that elementary school children in Brazil and in the United States understand and use one of the basic principles implicit in the manipulation of equations and that they can use nonconventional notation that helps them in solving algebraic problems. It was time, then, to evaluate whether they could understand and represent other core algebraic concepts and notation. Yet, we were very much aware that what children can do in individual interviews might not directly translate into what they can do in the classroom setting. Thus, if we were to evaluate the possibility of introducing algebra at the elementary school level, we needed to analyze children's abilities in the classroom, as they interact with a teacher who guides them in the development of new understandings and notations.

At this point, our ideas about what should constitute an algebrafied arithmetic curriculum pointed to the study of arithmetic operations as functions as the most promising path to follow. This is a rather daring proposal that needs to be tested in the classroom. Our questions, which are probably the questions many teachers and researchers must raise were: How could this be done? And how would children react and participate in such activities?

In the following chapters, we provide a few examples of how we introduced third graders to the ideas of addition and multiplication as functions. We show how, in both a classroom setting and in interviews, third graders participating in an exploratory Early Algebra study react to the activities and problems we created.

It is difficult to convey in words the classroom climate and the nature of students' engagement. Video clips may be more suitable for this. The CD-ROM companion to this book contains video clips to help the reader get a sense of the classroom conditions associated with chapters 4 through 6. They will help clarify what we mean by *treating arithmetical operations as functions.* And they contribute to the proof of existence claim about the capability of young students to understand algebraic relations and notation. Many readers may wish to view the videopapers in the companion CD before (or instead of) reading the text-only version of the chapters. The CDs contain both the chapter text and the videos, interactively linked. The videos can be viewed alone by opening the files chapter 4.mov, chapter 5.mov, or chapter 6.mov in a QuickTime Player.

Our data are part of a year-long classroom study. The school serves a diverse multiethnic and racial community. We undertook the work to understand and document issues of learning and teaching in an "algebrafied" (Kaput, 1998) arithmetical setting. Our activities in the classroom consisted of teaching a total of 15 Early Algebra lessons, 6 in the fall and 9 in the spring term.

The topics for the class sessions evolved from a combination of the curriculum content, the teacher's main goals for each semester, and the questions we brought to the table. We seized on additive comparisons as a special opportunity for approaching arithmetic from an algebraic standpoint during the six lessons we developed and implemented in the fall term. The nine lessons implemented in the spring focused on addition and multiplication as functions. Our previous research on everyday approaches to multiplication problems inspired our initial analysis of multiplication as a function, but soon other approaches came into play in the classroom. As we guided the students to go beyond their initial intuitive approaches, we introduced algebraic notations and focused our analysis on how this new tool helped children display and develop algebraic understandings.

4

Addition Operations
as Functions[6]

We believe, as others do, that many of the difficulties students have with algebra arise from the fact that algebra has been kept out of the early mathematics curriculum (see, e.g., Booth, 1988, and Kaput, 1998). But it would be naïve to hope that the situation could be improved simply by adding algebraic content and methods to current curricula. As we already stressed in this book, the real challenge consists in finding opportunities for bringing out the algebraic character of elementary mathematics. Arithmetic is a part of algebra. As such, arithmetic topics should be approached as instances of more abstract ideas and concepts. This will not only enrich children's understanding of arithmetic, but will also build the foundations for the meaningful learning of more advanced algebra in later years. This shift towards an algebrafied arithmetic could include various, possibly overlapping approaches, such as: generalizing arithmetic; moving from particular to generalized numbers; focusing on mathematical structures common to sets of algorithms; introducing variables and covariation in word problems; and re-

---

[6]This chapter is based on a Plenary Address delivered to the XXII Meeting of the Psychology of Mathematics Education, North American Chapter, Tucson, AZ, October 8, 2000, and on Carraher, D. W., Schliemann, A. D., & Brizuela, B. M. (2005), Treating operations of arithmetic as functions. *Journal for Research in Mathematics Education*, Monograph XIII, on CD ROM.

organizing curricula around abstract concepts that offer the possibility of uniting a range of topics that currently stand isolated in the curriculum, such as the concept of *function*. As we showed in chapter 1, there is some degree of consensus that algebraic reasoning belongs to the early mathematics curriculum. The question for many educators and curriculum developers becomes: What does this mean for the topics *already* in the curriculum? Presuming that many of the time-honored topics of early mathematics (number sense, addition, subtraction, multiplication, division) will stay around, what will they look like with their new, *algebrafied* personalities? What shifts in classroom activities are likely to occur as a result of elevating the importance of making generalizations? What opportunities for exploring the potentially algebraic character of standard school mathematics have been overlooked in the past? And how might they now be seized on so that young students can cultivate ways of reasoning that will prove useful not only now, but also much later when dealing with even more advanced mathematical ideas? Because changing the nature of the early mathematics curriculum only makes sense if it effectively helps students learn mathematics better and more deeply, we need research that looks into how students (and teachers) deal with standard topics presented in new ways.

Here, we focus on a remarkably simple idea: that the operations of arithmetic can be treated as functions in early mathematics education. Admittedly, some prominent mathematics educators have argued for the importance of functions in the mathematics curriculum, although only well after the elementary school years (e.g., Schwartz & Yerushalmy, 1992b; Yerushalmy & Schwartz, 1993). Others have defended the general goal of "algebrafying" early mathematics (Kaput, 1998). However, the field has largely failed to note that addition, subtraction, multiplication, and division operations can be treated from the start as functions, and that this idea could provide an important foothold for early algebra reform in current curricula.

In this and the next two chapters we describe some results from the year-long, third-grade teaching experiment we carried out in a classroom of 18 third-grade students at a public elementary school in the Boston area. The study aimed at understanding and documenting issues of learning and teaching in an "algebrafied" arithmetical setting (see Carraher, Schliemann, & Brizuela, 1999 and Kaput, 1998). The school where the classroom is set serves a diverse multiethnic and multiracial community, reflected well in the class composition, which included children from South America, Asia, Europe, and Central America. Our activities in the classroom consisted of teaching 15 90-minute Early Algebra lessons. The topics for the class sessions evolved from a combination of the curriculum content, the teacher's main goals for each semester, the questions we brought to the table regarding our research, and the interests, revelations, and confusions put forth by the children in our classrooms. We were well aware of the relative difficulty of additive comparison problems and seized on additive comparisons as a special opportunity for approaching arithmetic from an algebraic standpoint in the six lessons we developed and implemented in the fall term. The nine lessons implemented in the spring term focused on additive and multiplicative operations as functions.

In this chapter, we present examples of students taking part in activities regarding additive functions in the classroom and in an end of the fall term interview. The examples were chosen to show instances of children's algebraic reasoning as well as the challenges they face as they are asked to focus on functional relationships and to use letters to represent functional relations. Special attention will be given to the tension we identified in children's development as they deal with number relations and contextual constraints that are inherent to problem solving activities.

A BARE BONES EXAMPLE

One of the best-kept secrets of early mathematics education is that addition is a function or, at least, it can be viewed as a function. Clearly, nothing obliges us to treat addition as a function. Some would argue that it is sufficient to treat addition as a binary operation between numbers.[7] This is precisely how students are introduced to addition and subtraction when they learn, for example, that 3 + 5 yields 8 or that, if Samantha has three candies and gets five more candies, she will have eight candies. To view addition as a function requires that addition be treated as an operation on a *set of numbers or quantities*. Offhand, this might seem hopelessly foreign

---

[7]We are using the term number in a broad sense to include both *pure* numbers and those associated with physical quantities.

to the thinking of an 8- or 9-year-old child. However, it pays to look at what children themselves can tell us about the issue.

The following episode concerns our eighth lesson, in which students were filling out values for different cells in tables. In the previous week, we had worked with the class on activities related to function tables (these are described later in chaps. 5 and 6). During the seventh class, and at the beginning of the eighth class, we realized that students were filling out data tables correctly but without focusing on what we considered to be the essential relations among the values, or at least not construing the relations as we did. The instructor, David, therefore decided to play a number game that would introduce the convention for mapping values from one set onto another.

At this point the reader has the choice of reading the following transcription of the classroom discussion or of actually seeing the classroom interaction in the video clip that is part of the CD accompanying this book. We highly recommend closing the book and opening up the CD. As the video clips are part of a video paper, the rest of the chapter (and the next two chapters) can be read and seen from the CD.

David:	Let's work backwards.
Students:	Yeah!
David:	We'll start from the numbers, and then you tell me what the rule is. Can you, can you do that?
Students:	Yes!
David:	All right, I'm going to start; I'm not going to tell you what the rule is. Hold on, um. I'm going to start with 3. Hold on, hold on. Then I'm going to go to there, to 6. Paying attention? OK, and now, if I start from 7, I'm going to go to 10.

As the discussion progresses, the video clip shows David writing the number pairs on the board (see Fig. 4.1):

Student:	Um, can I tell you the rule?
David:	Does anybody have the rule figured out? If I start from 5, I'm going to go to . . .
Student:	8.

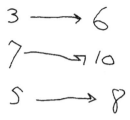

FIG. 4.1.   Input and outputs for $n \to n + 3$.

David: Yes, it will go to 8. [Laughs], I think somebody knows the rule. [Sara, raising her hand, is aching to be called on.] Jennifer, what were you thinking, what's the rule?

Jennifer: Plus 3?

David: Yeah, if I start from n, then I have to go to what?

Student: Plus 3.

David: 3?

Student: You have to *add* 3.

David: I have to add three to what?

Student: To the n.

David: Yes, to the n. So how am I going to write that down?

Students: n plus 3.

David: Yeah, that's the rule! [Writes $n \to n + 3$]

Student: Oh, we need something harder than that!

David: You need something harder?

Student: Yeah!

What are the children showing us they understand? For one thing, they seem to take the rule, "n becomes $n + 3$" as applying to all three of the cases that were presented. Hence n does not stand for a particular number but rather for *each and every* number that might serve as input.[8] N is understood to be a variable.

We do not wish to transmit the impression that the notation, $n \to n + 3$, was spontaneously invented by the students. As we see later, before this

---

[8]One of the children actually suggested, later in the class, that we refer to the terms on each side as *in* and *out*; we did so, and quickly moved to the expressions *input* and *output* to characterize the values of the domain and the values of the image, respectively.

class we had worked with students on developing notations for variables. They were already familiar with the convention of using a letter to stand for an undetermined value—"any number"—although they may have been considering the letters mostly as unknowns. But now, they were being asked to use it in a shorthand notation that expresses a whole set of values before and after a rule is applied, that is, as a variable. Clearly, the instructor plays a significant role in the interaction just discussed. When one student describes the rule as "plus three," the instructor seizes on the opportunity to focus on the names of values before and after the application of the rule. When the teacher refers to the input value as n, the original suggestion, "plus three," seems somehow inconsistent. So the students suggest amending the output value to "n plus 3." The transition from understanding letters as unknowns, to understanding them as variables is notoriously difficult, even for adolescents. However, in the video clips we see third graders transitioning from the use of unknowns to the use of variables. This becomes even clearer if we look more closely at the reasoning one of the students volunteered about this rule in the next clip.

David:	How about this one?
Melissa:	Because you have, well, you can say you have 10 then you add 3 more, and which, I mean, you have 11 then you add 3 more, equals 14. Yeah and say if you needed a 12, that equals 15.
David:	Hold on, 12 becomes 15. Yes, that's correct.
Melissa:	And I think the higher we go, the higher the numbers get, and . . .
David:	That's right. So could you do 100?
Students:	103.
David:	That's great, this is really neat.
Melissa:	And if you do 1,000, you get 1,003.
David:	Okay.
Student:	1 million, 1 million and 3.

Melissa's first offers the cases of 11, then 12, and then attempts to generalize: "the higher we go, the higher the numbers get." This suggests that she is referring to two *sets of numbers*, the numbers chosen ("the higher we go") as well as the numbers that emerge from applying the rule ("the higher the numbers get"). The numbers are connected one-to-one as ordered pairs; for each input number there is a respective output number. But she can also mentally scan the diverse cases in an ordered fashion and think about how variations in input are related to variations in output. The numbers covary according to a remarkably simple pattern: As input values increase, the output values increase, with the constraint that the latter are in every case precisely three units more than the former.

Melissa and the children around her understand that the rule can apply not only to the specific values chosen earlier, but also to numbers not previously considered. One suspects that, had they been asked, they would have considered the rule applicable to all (natural) numbers.

Such an example convinced us that young children can begin to think about addition and subtraction as additive functions and to understand and use algebraic notation, such as $n \to n + 3$. But we need to recognize this is a *bare bones* example. Only the most essential information is given: input and output numbers. No physical quantities are referred to, no worldly, out-of-school context need be considered. Let us now turn our attention to some examples from previous work (fourth lesson) with the same class, when we introduced the idea of additive functions embedded in word problems.

ADDITIVE FUNCTIONS AND WORD PROBLEMS

Certain conditions must be met for an applied context to represent a simple additive function such as, $n \to n + 3$. Both the variable element (n) and the constant element (3) must correspond to measurable *physical quantities*, sometimes referred to as *concrete numbers* (Fridman, 1991), as opposed to *disembodied, pure numbers*. They also must be of the same nature: for example, if n represents length then 3 must also represent (a particular) length. Furthermore, since n is variable, the rule ($n \to n + 3$) must credibly encompass a set of cases or instances.

In our work with second- and third-grade pupils, we have worked with three sorts of contexts—ages, money, and heights. Let us now look at some of the issues that came to the fore as students worked with additive functions involving heights.

It might seem odd to introduce heights as a context for an additive function. After all, people grow at different rates throughout their lives. But suppose the problem-poser *tells us* that there is a particular difference in the heights of two children at a certain moment in time, say, that Frank is 2 inches shorter than Jamie. If we have no other information, we can deduce neither of the children's heights. However, we do know the *difference* in their heights, and from that difference we can generate a set of *possible* solution pairs. We can vary Frank's height (since it is not fixed, it is free to vary), for example, and look at what each case would imply about Jamie's height. Whereas a problem about ages can be considered as a *change function*—variation reflects presumed changes in physical quantities over time—a problem about heights has a different character. Each pair of heights is a legitimate mathematical answer to the problem. However the data collection does not capture different states of a single phenomenon over time. In fact, if we restrict ourselves to a single moment in time, as the problem seems to require, then *at most* one case could be true (a person can have only one height). For such reasons, we might refer to the heights problem as a *multiple scenarios* function.

We posed a problem of this sort to our class of third grade students (see Fig. 4.2) in order to see whether they would treat it as a case of an additive function. At the beginning of the fourth class, the problem was shown to the children via projection onto a large screen. The children clearly understood that the problem entailed the heights of three children. However,

Tom is 4 inches taller than Maria.
Maria is 6 inches shorter than Leslie.
Draw Tom's height, Maria's height,
and Leslie's height.
Show what the numbers 4 and 6
refer to.

Maria   Maria's height

FIG. 4.2.   The "heights problem" as presented to the students.

several of the students initially understood the numbers to represent total heights. ("Tom is four inches tall . . .".)

One of the reasons we devised this problem was to create conditions that might discourage the students from solving problems by quickly performing computations on the numbers without thinking about the relationships between the physical quantities referred to in the problem. Because the heights of the characters could not be determined from the information given in the problem, we reasoned they would be forced to focus on the additive relations rather than perform computations on particular heights.

We wish to draw attention to two findings, each of which bear on the issue at hand, namely, treating addition and subtraction as additive functions. The findings concern the students' proclivity to instantiate with single values, and the use of algebraic notation.

Instantiation

Although we viewed the problem as open to many possible solutions, the students were initially inclined to seek out a single solution. In fact, their first reading of the problem led them to use the numbers given in the problem as the heights (in inches) of the children in the story. These sorts of reactions are understandable given the students' prior history with word problems, which they could solve by adding or subtracting, paying minimal attention to the words and context, and to the relations between the different numbers in the problem.

One child decided that Maria must be 6 inches tall and Leslie was 12 inches tall. Another volunteered that Tom was 10 inches tall, after adding 6 plus 4, the two numbers given in the problem—although he was puzzled by how a child could be so short. The problem gave information about *differences* between heights but the children initially treated the difference information as *actual heights*. (This shift in level of discourse calls to mind what Thompson, 1991, noted among fifth grade students, who mistakenly treated second-order differences as first-order differences.) As an attempt to get the children thinking about *differences* between heights, we decided to enact the problem in front of the class with three volunteers. In the course of this acting out, the three actors (students representing the people in the problem) helped the class gradually recognize the correct order of the children in the problem.

When the pupils had established a consensus about the relative order of heights of the three protagonists, we asked them to provide us with notations showing the information from the problem, and to try to indicate where the numbers "4" and "6" should "go" in their diagrams.

When they were asked to represent the children in a drawing, 12 of the students (66%) assigned a value, in inches, to each member of the story, even though nothing in the problem suggested that. The diagram in Fig. 4.3 typifies this. Note that "6" is taken to be Maria's height. The student instantiated the lengths—that is, assigned them particular values. Nonetheless, the differences between the heights of the three persons in the story are consistent with the information given in the problem.

Although only two numbers were given in the problem, every student who assigned values to heights provided three numbers, one each for Tom, Maria, and Leslie. In two cases, children wrote several numbers next to the children's height-arrows, as if they were writing numbers on a ruler. In seven of the twelve cases, children provided heights for Leslie, Tom, and Maria that were consistent with the numbers given in the problem. However, they did not label any parts of heights or intervals between heights as corresponding to these values. Even as they eventually

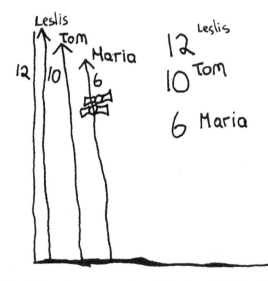

FIG. 4.3. Melissa's representation of the three heights whereby she instantiates each height.

came to realize that the measures—4 inches and 6 inches—referred to something other than total heights, many did not associate these values[9] with particular features of their diagram. The remaining six children (of the total of 18) did not assign particular heights. It is not clear whether this indicates that they realized that multiple possibilities existed, that they lacked the correct information, or that they simply decided not to include particular numbers. In the following episode, Kevin explains how he determined the heights.

Kevin:　　So she's (Leslie) taller than Tom by 2 inches. Mmhumm . . . cos Tom's taller than Maria by 4 inches . . . Mmhumm . . . and Maria is taller than, and Leslie is taller than Maria by 6 inches so that means that if he's taller than her by 4 inches and she, then Leslie has to be taller than Tom by 2 inches.

Bárbara:　　Mm . . . and to figure that out do you need to know exactly how high each one is?

Kevin:　　Yes

Bárbara:　　You do? How did you do it if you don't know how high they are?

Kevin:　　I do . . . cuz Maria's . . . Maria's . . .

Bárbara:　　Tell me exactly how high they are.

Kevin:　　Maria's . . . 4 feet 6 inches . . . and uh . . .

Bárbara:　　Where did you get that from?

Kevin:　　I don't know it just looks like that.

Bárbara:　　I think, I think you're just inventing that.

Kevin:　　I am.

Kevin correctly infers the difference between Tom and Leslie's heights to be equal to 2 inches. He instantiated Maria's height to 4 feet 6 inches (was this another way to get the numbers 4 and 6 into the problem?). His first answer is perfectly consistent with the data, but it suggests that he was not treating the heights as variable quantities but instead as unknowns.

---

[9]Adults understand that 4 inches corresponds to that part of Tom's height that surpasses Maria's height (i.e., lies above her head). Even when the children understood that 4 inches was "how much bigger" Tom was than Maria, they tended to indicate where this value lay (4 inches) by pointing to the top of each head. They did likewise when showing the "difference" between their own classmates' heights. For many, a difference could not be shown as an interval along a spatial dimension; one had to reenact the action of comparing!

Most of the other students seemed to approach the problem in this same way, at least until a function table was introduced.

Students' Use of Algebraic Notation

When the children had comfortably distinguished between heights and differences in heights, we asked them to consider several scenarios or "stories," each corresponding to a distinct row in the table we provided (see Fig. 4.4).

Row 1 gave Tom's height as 34 inches. Row 2 presents his height as 37 inches. We explained to the students that both stories could not be true at the same time and that these were two possible cases among many others. Maria and Leslie were each assigned heights of 37 inches in Stories 3 and 4, respectively. In the final story, Tom's height was listed simply as "T," which *we* took to refer to Tom's height, *whatever* it might be. As far as we can tell, this was the first occasion in which the children were shown letters standing for unknown measures. After some initial discussion, students quickly caught on to the idea that the first four stories were mutually exclusive: that is, at most, one of them could be true. Within a few minutes they were able to determine heights consistent with the relative information provided at the beginning of the class. Our attention then turned to Story 5, which, in *our* eyes, was a generalized description of each of the previous stories.

We intended that Story 5 be thought of as a general case (despite being called "Story 5") and we hoped that the students would be able to express Maria and Leslie's heights with respect to T, which we explained as standing for "Tom's height, whatever that might be." Most students found this puzzling, and several suggested calling Maria and Leslie's heights "M" and

What if...	Tom	Maria	Leslie
Story 1	34 in.		
Story 2	37 in.		
Story 3		37 in.	
Story 4			37 in.
Story 5	T		

FIG. 4.4.   A table of possible heights.

"L," respectively. Indeed, if the convention was to use the first letter of Tom's name to indicate his height, it made perfect sense to do likewise for the other two children. Others suggested that Maria and Leslie's heights should also be designated as T, arguing that T could stand for any height.

When we pointed out that assigning T to Maria's height would mean that Tom and Maria were of the same height, the students tended to realize that this might lead to a misunderstanding. The conversation then switched to the issue of "what we should call four less than T?"

Kevin filled in the table (see Fig. 4.5), concluding that in each story Maria was 4 inches shorter than Tom. In the final case, where Tom's height was given as T, after some prodding from the interviewer, he noted that in each story Maria was 4 inches shorter than Tom, which he expressed as "$T - 4$." Kevin then concluded that Leslie's height could be described by "$T + 2$."

After such a remarkable achievement—after all, it was Kevin's first use of algebraic notation to describe a word problem—we asked him to explain his reasoning to the rest of the class. His explanation shows him trying to find words for this new notation (note, for instance, the interpretation of T as "tall"):

> Tom is 4 inches taller than Maria.
> Maria is 6 inches shorter than Leslie.

Fill out the table for Story 1.
Imagine Tom is 34 inches tall. How tall will Maria and Leslie be?

What if...	Tom	Maria	Leslie
Story 1	34 in.	30 in.	36 in.
Story 2	37 in.	33 in.	39 in.
Story 3	41 in.	37 in.	43 in.
Story 4	35 in.	31 in.	37 in.
Story 5	T	T-4	T+2

Then work out the answers for Stories 2, 3, and 4.

FIG. 4.5. Kevin's answers for various scenarios or "stories."

Kevin: Oh, OK, tall. Tom's taller than Maria by 4 inches, and tall plus 2
               equals . . . Leslie's taller than Tom by 2 inches [writing $T + 2$ for
               Leslie].

Kevin's use of the letter T is reminiscent of other students' use of n to
stand for "none," "9," or for "19." Perhaps it felt strange to describe Leslie
according to a letter that stood for another student's name. It may have
been more helpful to use a letter such as x that does not seem intimately associated with one character in the story. In fact, two other children correctly solved the general case but, when asked what T stood for, gave
"tall" and "10" as possible interpretations. We tried to explain that T could
stand for "whatever Tom's height might be." This did not settle the issue,
though, but over the next several classes we found students increasingly
using the expression "any number" to explain the meaning of letters.

HOW DO THE ABOVE EXAMPLES BEAR
ON EARLY ALGEBRA?

The examples just discussed illustrate some issues characteristic of initial
learning in early algebra. We introduced the problem, "the heights problem," designed to represent a multiplicity of possible cases—in our view,
all cases for which there were differences of 2, 4, and 6 inches between the
heights of three children. The students initially tended to treat the values as
referring to *heights* instead of *differences*. The concept of an additive difference is in itself a challenging concept, one that has to be worked out for
a wide variety of mathematical contexts. This issue must be contended
with before any significant progress can be made on it.

Students preferred to represent the problem by assigning specific values
to various entities in the problem (the heights of the protagonists). We suspect that many adults would also proceed in a similar manner. Nonetheless, special efforts need to be made to ensure that students appreciate the
general character of the problem. In the present case, we tried to highlight
this fact by having students fill in a table that covered various scenarios. In
a sense, we tried to lend support to the idea that the problem was not about
any particular story, but rather about a host of stories consistent with the
information given. With similar intents, we introduced letters to stand for

unspecified quantities. Such emphases do not settle the issue once and for all. We were asking the children to construe problems as general ones even though they knew that any individual only has a particular height. This tension between the individual instances and general relations becomes more clear in the following example, in which we interviewed children about issues related to the mathematical content of the different lessons, during the 6th and 7th weeks of our study.

The interviews served as an additional source of data as well as an opportunity for the children to develop a greater understanding of problems similar to those presented in class. By then, the students had become noticeably familiar with additive differences. Their understanding of variables, as opposed to unknowns, was still under development, though, as the following interview excerpt reveals.

We entered the interview precisely when two pupils, Jennifer and Melissa, were discussing a height problem in which Martha was said to be 3 inches taller than Alan. David, the interviewer, focused on the expression "$x + 3$." (The following interaction is included on the companion video.)

David: Why were we using x's?

Jennifer: You might think like the x is Alan's height and it could be *any* height.

This would seem to suggest that Jennifer has settled the basic idea of what a variable is. But shortly thereafter it became clear that there were still matters to consider.

David: OK, now, if I didn't know Alan's height, and I just had to say, "Well, I don't know it so I'll just call it 'x.' . . ."

Melissa: You could guess it.

Jennifer: You could say like, well it would just tell you to say *any* number.

David: Why don't I use an x and say whatever it is I'll just call it x? [Umm.]

Both: [Puzzlement.]

David: Do you like that idea, or does that feel strange?

Jennifer: It feels strange.

Melissa: No, I pretty much . . . [unlike her classmate, she is comfortable with using *x* in this manner].

David: [addressing Jennifer] It feels strange?

Jennifer: Yes, 'cause it has to, it has to have a number. 'Cause . . . Everybody in the world has a height.

Jennifer seemed to think that it would be inappropriate to use the letter *x*, representing *any* height, to describe Alan because Alan cannot have *any* height; he must have a particular height. The interviewer moved to another example in the hopes that Jennifer would accept using the letter *x* to stand for a variable quantity.

David: Oh . . . OK. Well, . . . I'll do it a little differently. I have a little bit of money in my pocket. OK [to Jennifer], do you have any coins, like a nickel or something like that?

Jennifer: All mine's in the bag [in the classroom] . . .

David: OK, I'll tell you what: I'll take out, I'll take out a nickel here, OK. And I'll give that to you for now. I've got some money in here [in a wallet] can we call that *x*? [Hmm.] Because, *whatever it is*, it's that, it's the amount of money that I have.

Jennifer: You can't call it *x* because it has . . . if it has some money in there, you can't just call it *x* because you have to count how many money [is] in there.

David: But what if you don't know?

Jennifer: You open it and count it.

Jennifer insisted that it would be improper to refer to the money in the wallet as *x* because it holds a particular amount of money. (Melissa, who likens the value of *x* to "a surprise," experiences little, if any, conflict; *x* is simply a particular value that one does not know.) In a sense, Jennifer found the example inconsistent with the idea of *x* as a variable, that is, something capable of taking on a range of values. And she had a point: there is something peculiar about the fact that a variable stands for many values, yet we exemplify or instantiate it by using an example for which only one value could hold (at a time). She eventually reduced her conflict by treating the amount of money in the wallet as, hypothetically, able to take on more than one value:

Jennifer: The amount of money in there is . . . *any* money in there. And after . . . if you like add 5, if it was like . . . imagine if it was 50 cents, add 5 more and it would be 55 cents.

Here Jennifer seems to have adopted the interviewer's perspective, accepting to treat the amount under discussion as a variable as she considered different amounts that the wallet could have (in principle) held.

LESSONS FOR EARLY ALGEBRA

Elementary algebra can be viewed as a generalization of an arithmetic of numbers and quantities. Among the types of generalization we would like to draw attention to are: (a) statements about sets of numbers (e.g., "all even numbers end in an even digit") as opposed to particular numbers; (b) general statements about operations and functions (e.g., "the remainder of integer division is always smaller than the divisor"), as opposed to particular computations; and (c) expressions that describe relations among variables and variable quantities (e.g., "$y = x + 3$") as opposed to relations among particular magnitudes.

In this chapter, we described an attempt to closely document how young learners reason about problems of an algebraic or generalized nature.

In the "heights problem," the letters T, M, and L represent the people in the problem, their particular heights, and any and all possible values their heights might take on. Although the problem was grounded in a story about particular actors, the real story is about the relations among them, regardless of their particular values. The whole point of using multiple stories or scenarios in the classroom example was to draw attention to the invariant properties of the problem as the heights of individuals took on different values (varied).

The children in the study had to deal with the fact that the quantitative relations referred to *particular* numbers and measures on one hand (and in that sense were arithmetical), and were meant to express *general* properties not bound to particular values, on the other (and in this sense were algebraic). Reasoning about variable *quantities* and their interrelations would seem to provide a stage on which the drama of mathematical variables and functions can be acted out. However, using worldly situations to model mathematical ideas and relations presents students with challenging issues. On some occasions children may be inclined (as Kevin was) to instantiate variables—to assign fixed values to what were *meant* to be variable quantities—without recognizing their general character. On others, they may find it strange (as Jennifer at one point did) to use particular instances to represent variables and functions when any instance is of a constant, unvarying nature.

STRUCTURE VERSUS CONTEXT

In setting out to implement this classroom study, there were times when we wondered whether the main thesis was obvious. Who could possibly fail to notice the relevance of the operations of multiplication and addition to a function such as $3x + 7$? After all, these are the very operations one uses to produce output values from input values!

After one has studied functions, such ideas may indeed appear self-evident. But we need to look at the issue not from our own present, adult perspective, but rather from the perspective of learners and teachers in early mathematics instruction. Whereas in curricula about functions there are abundant references to the role of arithmetical operations, the reverse is not true. Many mathematics curricula designed for young learners contain little material that evokes the concept of function. We do not mean simply that the term, *function*, does not appear. Rather, operations tend to be treated solely as procedures for acting on individual numbers.

In treating arithmetical operations as functions, one encourages students to consider and formulate succinct descriptions of *patterns in sets of numbers*. These patterns manifest themselves in the repeated actions of students: students carry out the same computational routines on each and every numerical input. One can also view the patterns lying in the numbers themselves. However, there are many ways to read off or interpret number patterns. Natural language is students' first recourse for this task. However, algebraic notation allows students to capture these patterns in very succinct ways. Our initial results seem to suggest that young learners may be able to use such notation earlier than we had formerly suspected. The whole point of introducing algebraic notation early is not to accelerate children's movement across the vast spaces of the curriculum. Rather, it is more a question of making use of the opportunities for generalization that early mathematics affords. Early algebra is about teaching arithmetic and other topics of early mathematics more deeply, not about teaching algebra earlier.

Arithmetic is the science of number, but it also involves concrete numbers, and so, it is a science of quantities. What does this imply for early arithmetic and the algebrafication of arithmetic?

Our earlier studies of everyday mathematics (Nunes, Schliemann, & Carraher, 1993) suggested, time and time again, that rich, worldly contexts provided meaningful frameworks for children to learn about mathematical ideas. We noted how commercial transactions, for example, lent support to the underlying arithmetic (direct proportion, i.e., "the more you pay, the more you get," "change returned to a customer should always be less than the amount received," etc.). Further, street vendors naturally viewed multiplication through the building up of quantities in separate measure spaces (amount and price). We noted how, in contrast, multiplication routines taught in school tended to direct attention away from the worldly problem context and towards actions upon strings of digits. On several occasions, we criticized school approaches for ignoring the everyday mathematics children developed out of school. Perhaps we believed that school learning would ideally be closely grounded in children's everyday understandings.

However, we recognize that algebraic knowledge is not always grounded in thinking about quantities. There is a very legitimate sense in which algebra can be viewed as a syntactically guided manipulation of formalisms (Kaput, 1998). And there is a point where one can forget about the situations that gave rise to the algebra and extend one's knowledge within the rules of the algebraic symbolic system without having to return to the situations that originally gave meaning to the expressions (Resnick, 1986).

Our third grade students did seem to benefit from working with numerical relations unassociated with particular physical settings. Just as air tables simplify our reasoning about forces (by eliminating friction), function tables of pure numbers can expose the essential structure of mathematical relations.

But we must be careful not to be lured into viewing worldly contexts as mere distractions to mathematical problems (see Carraher & Schliemann, 2002a and Schliemann & Carraher, 2002). Do particular contexts and physical quantities merely provide noise that students must learn to filter out? We think not.

Much of the power and meaning of mathematics comes from our ability to apply it to a wide range of situations. This can only be achieved by working out the way in which mathematical concepts and representational tools relate to the particular characteristics of the situations. We must be careful not to dismiss the considerable effort students must make in such adaptations.

5

From Quantities to Ratio, Functions, and Algebraic Notation[10]

As we discussed elsewhere (Schliemann & Carraher, 2002), any analysis of how children develop mathematical knowledge must take into consideration the tools and representations they come to use and understand in everyday and in formal mathematics instructional activities. Children construct a foundation for logical and mathematical thinking on the basis of their direct experience and individual reflection as they participate in out-of-school activities. However, school classrooms are the privileged place where children are given access to mathematical tools and to experiences that will expand and strengthen their mathematical ideas. In attempting to fully understand the development of mathematical understanding, we need analyses of how children learn as they participate in school cultural practices, interact with teachers and peers in the classroom, become familiar with mathematical symbols and tools, and deal with mathematics across a variety of situations.

In this chapter we explore third graders' strategies for dealing with linear functions and constant rates of change, as they participate in Early Algebra

---

[10]This chapter is based on a Plenary Address delivered to the XXII Meeting of the Psychology of Mathematics Education, North American Chapter, Tucson, AZ, October 8, 2000, and on Carraher, D. W., Schliemann, A. D., & Brizuela, B. M. (2005), Treating operations of arithmetic as functions. *Journal for Research in Mathematics Education*, Monograph XIII, on CD ROM.

activities developed across two 90-minute lessons. As in chapter 4, the examples come from the same exploratory, year-long, third-grade teaching experiment we carried out in a classroom of 18 third-grade students at a public elementary school in the Boston area. Here we describe how we gradually adapted mathematical problems involving multiplicative linear functions, using function tables and algebraic notation to encourage children to describe functions with increasing clarity.

Our previous work on everyday mathematics suggests that informal mathematical learning and understanding can constitute a solid basis for the development of school mathematics and for the meaningful learning of conventional symbolic systems. However, a student's understanding of mathematics should not be restricted to his or her former everyday experiences. The field of mathematics, although indebted to its origins in farming and commercial activities, cannot be reduced to the circumstances that gave rise to its emergence (Schliemann, Carraher, & Ceci, 1997). This perspective undermines the argument that teachers should bring out-of-school activities to the classroom or that apprenticeship training should replace teaching (Carraher & Schliemann, 2002a; Schliemann, 1995).

The contribution of everyday mathematics to the learning of mathematics in school is not a matter of reproducing contexts, but rather a recognition that children bring to the classroom ways of understanding and dealing with mathematical problems that should be recognized as legitimate steps towards more advanced mathematical understanding. At the same time, we have to be aware of the differences between everyday approaches constructed as ways to reach everyday goals and the school mathematics goal of exploring multiple properties and representations of mathematical relations. This chapter explores the tension between third graders' own ways of solving problems and attempts to expand their understanding of proportionality, ratios, and linear functions.

FUNCTIONS AND RATE

Exploring children's conceptions of function and rate, specifically linear functions and constant rates of change, involves cases captured by notation such as "$y = mx + b$," where x and y are (independent and dependent) variables, m is a constant of proportionality, and b is the y-intercept when the function is graphed as a straight line in a Cartesian space. We all know that functions and rates involve considerably more than this. Yet mathematics educators differ widely about (a) what is critical to understand; (b) how instruction should proceed; and (c) how prior knowledge and experience play a role in understanding function and rate.

Students begin understanding (linear) functions and (constant) rates long before they make any sense of an expression such as $y = mx + b$. Educators effectively teach about functions and rates long before showing such expressions to students. Certain curriculum materials embody functional relations without making them explicit in algebraic notation. For example, a multiplication table might be thought of as an embodiment of the expression $y = mx$, where, x, y are integers along the margins and m corresponds to the number in the expression "times $<m>$ table." That mathematical concepts and ideas can be modeled, foreshadowed, dealt with intuitively, alluded to, and used as theorems in action (Vergnaud, 1994) constitutes an important fact of life in mathematics instruction, as well as an important focus of research. It also represents a significant departure from the view that mathematical concepts are best introduced by defining them precisely beforehand.

Studies of everyday mathematics show that quantities are crucial to the development of arithmetic concepts in the domain of additive structures. Quantities are also crucial in the development of concepts of function and rate, as well as to algebraic notation (Schwartz, 1996). Quantities serve as forerunners of mathematical variables, which are essential components of functions. One commonly thinks of quantities as "what you plug in for the value of x in an equation [of the family, $y = mx + b$] to get out a value for y." But this view leads to a conflation of concepts of quantity, number, and measure. In the realm of mathematics education (as opposed to mathematics) quantities are *inferred qualities* of objects, *inferred properties* of collections of objects and, in most cases, mental objects that can be acted on (Thompson, 1994). A person conceives of quantities when he or she views objects as capable of being ordered, counted, or measured along a continuum of possibilities. In this broad, psychological sense, quantities do not require numbers. This is precisely the view taken by Piaget to characterize a child's initial conception of speed as a "fastness" quality of objects (Piaget, 1970b). Much microcomputer-based laboratory work, such as that by Nemirovsky (1994), relies on the possibility of exploring functional relationships among quantities without requiring necessarily that students enter the world of numerical computation and additive measurement. One might also take a qualitative approach to situations where no explicit movement takes place: one can conceive of a specific door's width, for example, without measuring it or even having a particular unit of measure in mind.

By assigning numbers to quantities, either directly ("take 3 inches of rope"), or by computation or measurement, one produces measures, or measured quantities, and these representations, when given form in notation, contain information about both quantity (via a unit of measure) and number (how many units there are; Fridman, 1991). We believe that measures are very special mathematical objects, not only in everyday activities, but also in mathematics education, because they offer the opportunity for children to coordinate their experience with quantities and their emerging experience with numbers and number relations.

In planning to introduce multiplicative linear functions to the children participating in our classroom study, we started by building upon the results of everyday mathematics studies.

FUNCTION AND RATIO
IN NONSCHOOL SETTINGS

Let us quickly review how street sellers doing "oral mathematics" deal with quantities in situations that involve multiplicative relations (without tables) and how school children initially work with tables. Although these comparisons are not experimental, they nonetheless may serve a clarifying role.

When computing the price of a certain amount of the items they sell, street sellers start from the price of one item, usually performing successive additions of that price, as many times as the number of items to be sold (Carraher, Carraher, & Schliemann, 1985; Nunes, Schliemann, & Carraher, 1993; Schliemann, Araujo, Cassundé, Macedo, & Nicéas, 1998; Schliemann & Carraher, 1992; Schliemann & Magalhães, 1990; Schliemann & Nunes, 1990). Vergnaud (1983, 1988) described this strategy as a *scalar approach*. The main idea is that they tend to perform repeated additions along each variable, summing money with money, items with items. If we try to understand their procedure in terms of displacements in a function table, they work down the number column and the price column, performing operations on measures of like nature.

In contrast, a functional approach presumably relies on relationships between variables, often variables of different natures. This approach focuses on how one variable varies as a function of the other variable (Vergnaud, 1983). Although Greeks from antiquity used internal ratios widely, external ratios, and division of one measure by one of a different nature appeared in western mathematics only several hundred years ago (Freudenthal, 1983).

However, when we look carefully at the building up or scalar strategy found in everyday mathematics research, we realize that street sellers can establish a correspondence of values across measure spaces before proceeding to the next case. The flow of thought proceeds from one measure space to the other, row by row. This strategy is illustrated by the following solution by a coconut seller to determine the price of 10 coconuts at 35 *cruzeiros* each: "Three are one hundred and five, with three more, two hundred and ten (pause). There are still four. It is (pause) three hundred and fifteen (pause), it seems it is three hundred and fifty" (Nunes, Schliemann, & Carraher, 1993, p. 19). This mental computation solution strategy can be represented by the table and diagram in Fig. 5.1.

Sometimes street sellers may build up by successive doubling; for example, they may say, "3 cost 35, 6 cost 70, 12 cost 140" and so on, thus making use of the principle that $2 \times f(x) = f(2 \times x)$.

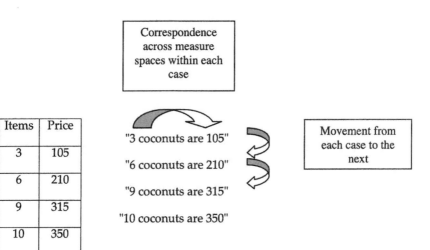

FIG. 5.1.   The scalar computation strategy.

Their scalar approach indeed involves a linking of a unique y-value to each value of x. It therefore captures the essential idea of a function, something easy to miss in accounts of building up and scalar solutions. However, this is appreciated in an intuitive sense and not expressed formally or generally by the street sellers; it thus constitutes an example of Vergnaud's (1994) theorem in action, as opposed to a theorem.

Scalar solutions and repeated addition of the price of one item has also been found among young school children (Kaput & West, 1994; Ricco, 1982). Thus, use of scalar solutions and of unit ratios may be a good start towards understanding functions, as Kaput and West (1994) proposed. We have to be aware, however, that the goal of school instruction is to lead students to focus on general relationships and develop general problem solving models and notation. We also have to consider the limitations of repeated addition as a step towards understanding multiplication (Thompson & Saldanha, 2000).

Scalar solutions may constitute a meaningful and efficient strategy to solve missing value proportionality problems, but it is limited in scope and typically does not allow for broader exploration of the relationships between the two variables. For example, if the starting amount is larger than the ending amount, street sellers fail to find solutions (Schliemann & Carraher, 1992). Moreover, when the relationship between price and number of items (the functional relation) is numerically "easier" (Greer, 1994) than the scalar relation, school children are more inclined to focus on the functional relation while street sellers continue to use the scalar computational strategy, even when this choice leads to more cumbersome computations (Schliemann & Carraher, 1992).

In this chapter we look at some specific examples of how third graders' emerging understanding of number relations draws on and at the same time departs from their previous school and out-of-school experiences with quantities and with numbers, as they participate in Early Algebra lessons that focus on ratios and functional relations.

THE INTERVENTION AND ITS RESULTS

Our goal in the set of lessons we describe in this chapter was to help children build an understanding of multiplication from an algebraic point of view and as a functional relationship. To reach this goal, we designed activities that aimed at shifting the focus from scalar relations to functional relations and to general algebraic representation. Soon, however, we realized that the children in our classroom were not using a scalar strategy at all. Instead, they would focus on each individual column pattern, completing them in isolation. Through a discussion of children's difficulties and successes as they participated in these activities, we explore some of the issues they faced in trying to move from their isolated column approaches to a functional approach, and from computations to generalizations.

We focus on situations in which quantities have already been associated with a certain number of units of measure. We highlight some issues students and teachers must deal with in using "multiplication problems" as a springboard for students' emerging understanding of ratio, proportion, and linear functions, and their growing ability to articulate these concepts in increasingly general language and algebraic notation.

Because we treat algebra as a generalized arithmetic of numbers and quantities, we view the transition from arithmetic to algebra as a move from thinking about relations among particular numbers and measures toward relations among sets of numbers and measures, from computing numerical answers to describing relations among variables. This approach requires providing a series of problems to students, so that they can begin to note and articulate the general patterns they see among (what we take as) variables. Tables play a crucial role in this process insofar as they allow one to systematically register diverse outcomes (one per row) and look for patterns in the results. Once the pattern has been understood, a student can fill in empty cells of the table based on their appreciation of the underlying function. Moreover, there are good reasons for encouraging students to explicitly formulate the relationship between measures, as opposed to merely giving a list of cases, each of which satisfies the function.

During the period of our investigation, the 18 third graders in the study were intensely working on learning the multiplication tables. In the 7th week of our intervention, we started working on multiplicative relations. Our first challenge at this point was to design situations that would allow children to understand multiplication as a functional relationship between two quantities.

Building on what we knew about street sellers and young children's strategies to solve price problems, we adopted this as a departure point. From our perspective, the organization of data for two related quantities in a table would presumably provide the opportunity for children to use their own scalar strategies but would also allow us to explore with them the implicit functional relationships between two variables. As children reacted to the tasks in unexpected ways, we realized that certain constraints and changes had to be introduced to allow children to focus on rate and functional relations. The sequence of tasks we designed to achieve our goals were presented and discussed over 2 meetings of 90 minutes each. The first two tasks were part of our first meeting and the other four were part of the second.

At this point, as was the case in the previous chapter, we strongly recommend that the reader close the book and open the CD to read the remaining of the chapter in video paper format, watching the classroom and interview videos, instead of reading the transcription of the conversations that took place as children were challenged to consider multiplicative functions and algebraic notation.

FIRST MEETING: CHILDREN'S INITIAL STRATEGIES

Task 1—Filling Out Function Tables

On the first day, we began by asking children to fill out the table shown in Fig. 5.2. Each child received a work sheet, but we suggested that they could work in pairs, discuss their solutions, and help each other.

The video clip transcribed in the following section shows the interaction between one of the researchers, Ana, and two of the children, Yasmeen and James. These children's solutions exemplify the initial approaches observed in the classroom.

Ana:	So, Yasmeen, did you see the problem? [Pointing to the first empty cell in the table.] What do you think should come in here?
Yasmeen:	One.
Ana:	Yeah, let's write it. Now, let's go to a more difficult one.
Yasmeen:	[Fills out all the empty cells in the first column.]
Ana:	Oh, that's clever, so now you have the numbers in the first column. So, one is 3, 2 is 6, how much should one pay for 3?

Mary had a table with the prices for boxes of Girl Scout cookies. But it rained and some numbers were wiped out. Let's help Mary fill out her table:

Boxes of cookies	Price
	$ 3.00
2	$ 6.00
3	
	$ 12.00
5	
6	
	$ 21.00
8	
9	
10	$ 30.00

FIG. 5.2. The incomplete table.

James:	Oh, I know this. This would be nine.
Ana:	That . . . OK . . . a nine, why do you think it's a nine? Explain it to Yasmeen.
James:	Because it's times like 3. Three, 6, 9, 12. And it goes on and on.
Yasmeen:	Yeah, because it's counting by threes.
Ana:	Yeah, so, would you fill it up the next one?
James:	15, 18.
Ana:	Very good.
James:	Hey! That's right in the book?
Yasmeen:	[Opens up her book and checks her multiplication tables and results of multiplying by three the numbers in the first column corresponding to empty cells in the second.]

Most of the students in the class, like Yasmeen and James, first appeared to treat each column, items and price, as separate problems. Yasmeen discovered that she could fill out column one by counting by 1s. James "solved the Column 2" problem by counting by 3s. Their isolated column approach leads to correct answers but it does not involve them in thinking about the general relationships between price and items. The diagram in Fig. 5.3 depicts the steps in their solution.

However, James has perhaps drawn Yasmeen's attention to multiplication through his remark, "You times by three." Once Yasmeen realized that the cookie-price table worked just like multiplying by three, she consulted her book to make sure her answers were in accordance with the multiplication table. Only a few children, like Yasmeen, related the task to the multiplication tables they were memorizing and used the latter to fill out the second column in the table.

Task 2—Different Ways to Go From One Number to Another

The remainder of this class was dedicated to an activity where the children had to find different ways to operate on a number in order to get to another (e.g., "How do you get from 2 to 8?" and "How do you get from 3 to 15?"). This activity constituted an attempt to have children exploring the multiple

Boxes of cookies	Price
1	$ 3.00
2	$ 6.00
3	$ 9.00
4	$ 12.00
5	$ 15.00
6	$ 18.00
7	$ 21.00
8	$ 24.00
9	$ 27.00
10	$ 30.00

FIG. 5.3.   James' and Yasmeen's strategy.

relationships between two numbers in a pair. We hoped that this would later help them to focus on determining the relationship in a function table.

The first and most popular solutions were additive solutions such as: "Add 6 to 2" or "Add 2, plus 2, plus 2." As discussions developed, however, children started using multiplication as an alternative way to get from one number to the other.

SECOND MEETING: DEVELOPING NEW STRATEGIES AND ALGEBRAIC NOTATION

Task 1—Focusing on Any Number (n)

The following week, we first presented children with a multiplication table similar to the one they had worked with, except for an added n row. Our goal here was to lead children to state the general relationship depicted in the table. They were asked the questions shown in Fig. 5.4.

1. Last week we filled out the table below.

But now there is an extra row.

What do you think the n means?

What is the price if the number of boxes is n?

Describe what happened.

Boxes of cookies	Price
1	
2	$6.00
3	$9.00
4	$12.00
	$15.00
	$18.00
7	$21.00
8	
9	$27.00
10	$30.00
N	

FIG. 5.4. Filling out a table and generalizing N.

Again, children easily filled in the blanks by counting by ones in the first column and counting by 3s in the second. David, the instructor for the two classes, asked them to explain how they found the number in the price column that corresponded to 4 boxes of cookies. One child responded that he added four threes. Regarding the second row, one child explained that it was 3 times 2 and another that one had to add 4 to 2. For the nth row one of the students, Sara, stated: "add 3 up; 11 times 3 equals 33; n probably stands for 11." Other children also considered that n was 11 and that the corresponding value in the second column was 33. As we see, even though attributing a specific value to n, the children were starting to consider how a number in the first column related to the number in the second.

David explained that "n stands for anything." A child stated: "It could be any number." After discussion and examples, three children maintained 33 as a response in their worksheets, three left the cell blank, five adopted $n + n + n$ or nnn as their response, and seven adopted the notation $3n$ or $n \times 3$. One girl wrote on her work sheet, the expression $n \times 3$ followed by the equals sign: "$n \times 3 =$."

Task 2—Breaking the Columns' Pattern

For the next task, we decided to make larger breaks in the table sequence hoping to further draw children's attention to the functional relationship across columns (see Fig. 5.5).

This table also introduced a more demanding relationship because it represented a function with an additive term $y = 2x + 1$. The following video clip and the transcript depict the interaction between one of the researchers (Ana) with Jessica and Sara, and then with Jennifer. It shows the children's struggles to solve the task.

Ana: [Approaching Sara and Jessica, who had already filled out their tables up to the 10th row but did not know what to do next] Let's see, if you times this number [pointing to 7] by something, how close does it get to 15?

Jessica: 20?

Ana: Let's see, if you say 7 times something. How close do you get to 15? If you do 7 times 2, how much do you get?

Jessica: 14?

Ana: To get to 15?

Jessica: You have to add 1.

Ana: You have to add 1. Let's think about that, you two. Would that same thing apply to the other numbers?

Jessica: Yeah.

2. Here is another table. Can you fill in the missing values?

X	Y
1	3
2	5
3	7
4	9
5	
7	
8	
9	
10	

20	

30	

100	

N	

FIG. 5.5. Filling out a table and generalizing to higher values and *N*.

Ana: Yeah? Show me for this one [pointing to 9], what happens to go from 9 to 19?

Jessica: 9 times 2.

Ana: Yeah, and then?

Jessica: Add 1.

Ana: Add 1. Let's see if it works for the other rows. What about this one [pointing to 3]?

Jessica: 3 times 2 add 1.

Ana: Ha-ha. So.

Jessica: OK, so, is it like, 10 times 2 is 20, add 1, 30! [Sic]

Ana: [Approaching Jennifer] So, what did you do, Jennifer? Let me see. Yes, you did up to here [Row 10]. Now, let's find out what the rule is, to get to this one, here (Row 20). 20. What's the number that should go there (in the y column for Row 20)? I was telling the girls there, that if you look here, how is it that you get from 3 to 7? If you multiply 3 by something . . .

Jennifer: 3 times . . . 3 times 2?

Ana: Yeah, how much do you get?

Jennifer: 3 times 2 is 6.

Ana: OK, but you need 7.

Jennifer: Oh, I know, 3 times 2 plus 1 equals 7. This [pointing to 4] is 4 times 3 [confusing times 2 for times 3, possibly because she started with the 3 × 2 example] is 8 plus 1 equals 7, plus 1 equals 9.

Ana: Yeah, yeah, so?

Jennifer: So 2 times 3 plus 1 equals 7, I mean . . . [remembering that she is referring to 20] 2 plus 3 . . . [confusing times for plus and 2 for 3] 20 plus 3 is 23, 24, here.

Ana: Let's see. If you do 2 times, as you were doing here [pointing to row above].

Jennifer: 2 times 3?

Ana: No. What were you doing here [pointing to 8]? Let's see . . . 8 times.

Jennifer: Oh, 8 times 2, plus 1.

Ana: OK. OK. So, if you do the same here [pointing to 20].

Jennifer: 20 times 2 is 40, plus 1 equals 41.

Ana: Yeah.

As we have just seen, for the more challenging relation between the two columns, the children did not spontaneously focus on the functional relationship and needed external help to complete the table. The task was clearly difficult to them, even if taken as a simple computational routine where the same rule had to be applied to the input in order to generate an output. At the end, however, with guidance and despite a few computational mistakes, they were able to apply the rule and to complete the table.

Task 3—Developing a Notation for the Function

The next step was to focus on a general notation for the function they worked with in the previous task. David wrote the rule $n \times 2 + 1$ on the board and worked with the whole class, assigning different values for n and computing the results. The same was done for $3n + 2$. He replaced n with different numbers, including 0 and 1,000, and children easily computed the output.

Task 4—Finding the Rule From Two Pairs of Numbers

For the next activity, David wrote on the board pairs of numbers and asked the children to find the rule that originated them. The first trial of this task was described in detail in chapter 4. As we then explained, in the first trial, David wrote 3 and 6 as a first pair and 7 and 10 as a second pair and the children easily found that they had to add 3 to the first number.

At the children's demand to give them "something harder," David wrote the number pairs shown in Fig. 5.6, one by one, and asked the children to guess the rule he was using.

The video clip transcribed below shows the enthusiastic participation of children in this rather challenging task:

David: I think I better give you another example [writes 5 as an input and 9 as an output]. Sara, you already want to try it?

[. . .]

David: OK. If I give you a 3, you've got to get a 5 out. You think you still know? You think you know, Michael?

Michael: Yeah.

David: If I gave you an n, then what, OK . . .

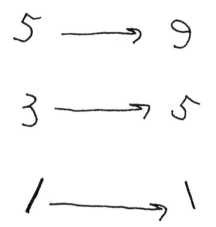

FIG. 5.6.   Input and outputs for $n \rightarrow 2n - 1$.

Michael: For the first one . . .

David: For the first one, how do you get from 5 to 9?

Michael: Add 4.

David: You add 4. And if I add 4 to 3?

Students: No.

David: You could've been right. Cause that's one way to get from 5 to 9 [adding 4]. However, this rule, it can't be that rule cause it didn't work for the second one [from 3 to 5]. Because if I added 4, this would become 7, and it became 5. Let me give you another example. If I give you a 1, do you know what you're gonna get from this?

James: Oh, I know!

David: James. Let's see if he's got it.

James: You have to add 2?

David: You add 2? So if you add 2 to 5 you get how much?

Student: 9.

David: No, you don't get 9.

Student: 7.

David: Actually, it's not as hard. If I give you a 1, you have to get out a 1.

Student: Oh, 1 times 1 equals 1.

David: One times 1 would be 1. But 5 times 5 isn't 9.

Jessica:	Sara knows!
David:	Sara, give us a, clarify for us.
Sara:	Two times that number minus 1.
David:	Wow! Wow! Sara, come here, write this up here. Write it up here, if you can generalize it.
Sara:	[Writes "$x \, 2 - 1$"].
David:	Write the n in front so we remember, n times 2 minus 1. Have you guys got this figured out? Did you see what she did? So you have to use which times table, Sara? This is really something!
Students:	Harder, harder.
David:	Pardon me?
Students:	Harder, harder.

Sara was the one who first found the rule. And it is likely that she was among a small minority of students who could infer a linear function from a series of instances. However, as we can see in the next video clip, once she gave the rule, the other students seemed to immediately recognize that it worked, and they eagerly took turns showing that they understood what was going on, as in Nathia's case:

| **Nathia:** | The number 2, you times it 2 more times, then you take away 1 and it ends up to 3. |
| **David:** | Right. You're explaining it the way Michael was explaining it. That's correct. So you times it times 2, whatever that number was, and then you take away 1. We're using now Sara's rule. |

Shortly after that, Jennifer walked up to David and whispered in his ear that he should work with the rule, "$4x + 4$." Once again, Sara solved the rule, and other students took turns explaining why the rule worked.

Our main point is not that students quickly and decisively mastered linear functions. We do wish to point out, however, that linear functions can begin to be explored as extensions to students' work with multiplication tables and with the operation of multiplication. Further, even though not all third grade students may identify the linear functions underlying data tables, they can learn significant things in the resulting discussions.

It should be further pointed out that, in her approach, Sara was probably considering the x as a variable, given her statement "2 times that number minus 1." By "that" number, we assume that Sara probably meant "any given number," and not a particular unknown.

DISCUSSION

We started our teaching intervention by using function tables relating two quantities: number of items and price. We found that although the children could correctly fill in the tables, they seemed to do so with a minimal of thought about the invariant relationship between the values in the first and second columns. Several didactical maneuvers were introduced in an attempt to break the students' habit of building up in the tables.

It was only when a guess-my-rule type of game was introduced that students were finally able to break away from the isolated column strategies they had been using. We are not certain why this occurred. One prominent feature of the "guess-my-rule game" was that there was no discernible progression in input values to subsequent input values. This is also what happens in everyday market situations where vendors compute individual prices and, in doing so, develop an understanding about the correspondence of values across measure spaces. If this is truly an important consideration, one would suggest that we introduce function tables without systematically ordering the rows from smaller to greater values.

In our everyday mathematics studies (Nunes, Schliemann, & Carraher, 1993), we found that contextualized problems are much easier to be solved than decontextualized problems. It may therefore seem surprising that third-grade children were content to work with pure numbers and numerical relations and used this context for extracting patterns and functional relationships. However, as we discussed elsewhere (Carraher & Schliemann, 2002a; Schliemann, 1995), what makes everyday contexts powerful is not the concreteness of the objects or the realism of the situations dealt with in everyday life, but the meaning attached to the problems under consideration. In this classroom, through the sequence of tasks and discussions we held with the children, we may have succeeded in creating meaning for problems that dealt exclusively with number relations. And this happened in a classroom of children from a multiethnic, multiracial neighborhood, many of them from recent immigrant families. The school ranks among those with low scores in the compulsory standard achievement tests imposed by the state. Despite these drawbacks, we found that the children could focus on functional relations if the tasks they are asked to solve are conducive to examining functional relations. They did not need concrete materials to support their reasoning about numerical relations and could even deal with notations of an algebraic nature. In fact, the introduction of algebraic notation helped them to move from specific computation results to generalizations about how two series of numbers are interrelated.

6

On Children's Written Notation to Solve Problems[11]

In traditional mathematics classes, setting written equations to solve problems and using the syntactic rules of algebra to solve them constitutes the core of algebra learning. Even though this vision of algebra is too restrictive and does not consider the many other features of algebra (see Kaput, 1998; Usiskin, 1988), we believe that algebra notation plays an important role in learning algebra and in solving algebra problems. As such, throughout our interview and classroom studies, analysis of children's notation has been a central focus of our analysis.

The interview data we analyzed in chapter 3 exemplify some of our first explorations of children's understanding and use of algebraic notation, and, in more general terms, of children's ways of representing their algebraic understandings and the algebraic problems they are presented with. It is clear that:

- Some children feel that they need to make notations for problems with numerical information but not for problems that deal with logical rela-

---

[11]This chapter is based on previous presentations by B. Brizuela, D. Carraher, and A. Schliemann at the Research Presession, 2000 Meeting of the National Council of Teachers of Mathematics, Chicago, IL, and at the Ninth International Congress of Mathematical Education, Tokyo-Makuhari, Japan, August 2000.

tionships; they prefer to solve problems about logical relationships among quantities "in their heads."

- Notation can do more than register the data in a problem and the operations to be performed.
- Notation can serve multiple roles such as to register and guide students' thinking, to keep track of different parts of a problem, and to help them find an answer to a problem.
- Children can combine both idiosyncratic and conventional notation in their representations.
- Conventional and algebraic notation can be used by children to further their understanding of problems and algebraic concepts.

Our classroom studies described in chapters 4 and 5 introduced children to conventional algebraic notation to represent variables. Brito Lima (1996; see also Brito Lima & da Rocha Falcão, 1997) and Bodanskii (1991) have already shown that written algebraic notation is within reach of elementary school children. In our teaching experiments we observed among our students the gradual way in which their notations become more and more context independent. At the beginning of the school year, the notations that children created to represent and solve algebraic problems were imbued with features peculiar to the problem at hand. For example, in representing a problem in which 17 fish had been reduced to 11 fish, children drew fish, with eyes, tails, and fins. Although these notations effectively served the purpose of representing the problem at hand, they would probably not effectively serve the task of representing problems with a similar underlying arithmetical structure, such as representing how a bank balance of 17 dollars fell to 11 dollars. As the weeks went by, however, the children's notations became ever more schematic and general, focusing on the logical relationships among quantities instead of the physical properties of the quantities themselves. In the two previous chapters, we also documented how the use of a letter to represent any number helped children in considering variables and functions.

In this chapter, we further explore children's notations as they participate in early algebra classroom activities and consider the role that written notation may play in children's thinking about different problems. In the back of our minds was constantly a question posed by Kaput (1991): "How do material notations and mental constructions interact to produce new constructions?" (p. 55).

In his work regarding cultural tools and mathematical learning, Cobb (1995) highlighted two opposing perspectives—the sociocultural and the constructivist—in the analysis of children's notations. One could argue from a sociocultural perspective that children internalize the algebraic notations used by the mathematical community. The other would argue, presumably from an extreme constructivist perspective, that conceptual development will occur independently of the cultural tools—such as algebraic notation—that learners make use of. Our position is midway between these dichotomous views. Therefore, our task is to explore and document how the assimilation of conventional algebraic notation interacts with both children's conceptual development regarding algebraic relations and their incipient and spontaneous ways of representing.

Our examples are taken from the same third-grade classroom we described in chapters 4 and 5. The specific examples we focus on refer to Sara. Sara exemplifies, through her actions and her words, how notations can represent not only what was done when solving a problem and what happened in the context of the problem (as we saw in chap. 3 with Eliza, Maggie, and Melanie), but also how notations can become tools for thinking and reflecting about the relationships between quantities in the problem (as happened with Charles, also in chap. 3). In this way, we can begin to think about children's notations not only as tools for learners to represent their understanding and thinking about algebraic relations or as precursors of conventional algebra representation, but also as tools to further those understandings and that thinking. As Sara explained to one of us during an interview, referring to the pie chart she had drawn to represent the fractions she was thinking about, "Well, I don't . . . when I draw this [the pie chart] it's just to help me think of something, so it doesn't really matter [if the pieces of the pie chart are different sizes]."

The episodes in this chapter are also included in the CD that accompanies the book. Therefore, once again we urge the reader to watch the video clips in the corresponding video paper, instead of reading the transcription of the episodes.

USING NOTATIONS TO SOLVE PROBLEMS

At our May 28th class, the fifteenth and last class meeting with us, David and our third grade students were solving fraction problems. The first problem presented to the class to think about is shown in Fig. 6.1.

As we had done many times before, we encouraged the students to use any kind of representation they felt comfortable with—arrows, shapes, drawings, or pie charts. In the week preceding this class, their regular classroom teacher had introduced the children to the use of pie charts as notations for unit fractions. As the students began to think about the problem in Fig. 6.1, Jennifer, a student in the class, proposed that the answer should be 24—that is, that the character in the problem must have started with 24 dollars. Explaining her solution by referring to *fourths* rather than *thirds*, she explained, "one fourth of it [the money she had] is 6 dollars, if you add 6 dollars four times it should be 24." Following this, David asked for more volunteers to explain how they understood the problem. The video clips of Sara solving this and other problems provide a good view of how she uses notations to solve the problems.

> **David:** [Sara put her hand up to participate.] OK. Sara, go ahead, show us what you're understanding.
>
> **Sara:** She [referring to Jennifer] said one fourth. But it [the problem] says one third. So you kind of draw it into parts like this, I mean like that [drawing a pie chart into thirds, with a number "6" written in each section of the pie, on the overhead projector].

Jennifer spent one third of her money to buy ice cream. After buying the ice cream, she ended up with $6.

How much money did she start with? How do you know?

Draw a picture showing:

Her money before buying ice cream

The money she spent for the ice cream

The money she had after buying the ice cream.

FIG. 6.1.   Problem presented to Sara and her peers during class.

David:	How many parts do you have there?
Sara:	3.
Michael:	[Referring to the pie chart cut into thirds.] That's a peace sign.
Sara:	6, 6, and 6 [pointing to the three "pie pieces" in her diagram]. So 6 and 6 is 12 [pointing to two pieces of her pie chart]. And 6 is 18 dollars all together [pointing to the last piece].
David:	So now we have two different answers [for the total amount of money the character in the problem had—24 and 18]. Go ahead.
Sara:	[Reading the problem on the projection screen.] One third of her money on ice cream. And . . . but . . . I did that wrong [going back to her notation of the pie chart].
David:	You did that wrong, why?
Sara:	Because it should be like this [crossing out her first notation and then drawing a pie chart into thirds, this time with number "3" written in each section]. Because if she has 9 dollars, this is her ice cream [pointing to one of the pieces or thirds], and then this is the 6 dollars that she ended up with [pointing to the two remaining pieces and referring to the 6 dollars mentioned in the problem]. If she spent this [pointing to one piece] for her ice cream, there's 3 and 3 [pointing to the two pieces of the pie chart that remained].
David:	So now you're thinking she might have had 9 dollars instead of 18. OK.

After having solved the problem in front of the whole class, she worked on her desk and produced, on paper, the notations shown in Fig. 6.2.

In this classroom example, we see Sara trying to figure out the problem she was presented with, and using the notations she makes to help her figure out her answer. While trying to solve the problem in front of the whole class, Sara first represented her thinking about the problem, what she thought the problem was stating. She did not attempt to represent the sequence of actions that took place in the problem—like the buying of the ice cream and the spending of the money.[12] Instead, she extracted the es-

---

[12]Sara's writing "left" and "ice cream" could be taken to represent the different actions in the problem. These particular notations, however, were not made while she was solving the problem, and seem to express the "types" of quantities (i.e., this is the money that was left over or the money that was spent) more than the different steps of the problem.

FIG. 6.2. Sara's notations for solving the ice cream problem.

sential information to be able to solve the problem and considered this information as a whole. In this, she differs strongly from Eliza (see chap. 3), who needed to represent the numbers in the problems in a sequence that corresponded to the actions described in each case.

The first issue to sort out in this problem was that of "the thirds," given that Jennifer had first represented the problem in terms of fourths. Then, as Sara reflected on the notation she produced—a pie chart divided into three pieces—she was able to return to the problem and think about it through the lens of the notation she had created. In returning and reflecting, she changed her thinking. She found that the first thirds' notation that she had made, with 6, 6, and 6, did not correspond to having two thirds of the amount being 6, as had been mentioned in the problem. So using this first notation as a springboard, she only had to make a minor adjustment to her initial notation to match what was going on in the problem. Although Sara was using the type of notation for fractions she was taught by her teacher, she was appropriating this particular notation and making use of it in a new way, to figure out the solution for a problem. In doing this, we may say that she was reinventing the notation.[13] Again, this is very different from Eliza's approach in Example 1. Eliza used her notations to represent all her *actions*, but she did not use them to show *relationships among quantities.*

Although using the pie chart to support her reasoning and problem-solving processes, Sara was developing a representation that is some-

---

[13]In fact, we found that the use of the pie charts to represent unit fractions did not necessarily help the children to solve or understand the different fraction problems. We are reminded here of E. Mach's (1906) point that "symbols which initially appear to have no meaning whatever, acquire gradually, after subjection to what might be called intellectual experimenting, a lucid and precise significance" (cited in Cajori, 1929/1993, p. 330). Symbols, such as the "pie chart" don't automatically lead to an understanding about fractions.

what similar to the line-segment diagrams proposed by Bodanskii (1991) and by Simon and Stimpson (1988) as a step towards students' development of algebraic representations. She used the pie and its three slices as placeholders for known and unknown amounts. The total unknown amount is a whole pie that is divided into three pieces of which two, taken together, represent 6 dollars. Although Sara did not need to write an equation to solve the problem, her approach depicts the basic structure of the relationships described in the problem and could become the foundation for an equation such as $3x - x = 6$ or $6 + x = 3x$, that could be used as a step towards the problem's solution.

USING NOTATIONS TO SHOW A SOLUTION

The following episode, from a later activity during that same class, illustrates once again how Sara was using the notation to think and reflect about the problem. The children had begun to work individually or in pairs on the problem shown in Fig. 6.3.

David noticed Sara's solution and notation for the problem (see Fig. 6.4) and called Analúcia over so Sara would explain her notations and her

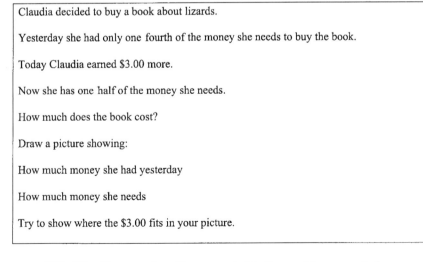

> Claudia decided to buy a book about lizards.
>
> Yesterday she had only one fourth of the money she needs to buy the book.
>
> Today Claudia earned $3.00 more.
>
> Now she has one half of the money she needs.
>
> How much does the book cost?
>
> Draw a picture showing:
>
> How much money she had yesterday
>
> How much money she needs
>
> Try to show where the $3.00 fits in your picture.

FIG. 6.3.   The second problem presented to Sara and her peers during class.

FIG. 6.4. Sara's notation for the book on lizards' problem.

thinking. The video clip transcribed in the following section provides a lively picture of her explanation:

Sara: I decided that . . . Claudia decided to buy a book about lizards. Yesterday she had only one fourth of the money she needs to buy the book [reading the problem]. When it said one fourth, I decided I'd draw the circle with the line and the line [referring to the pie chart and the vertical and horizontal lines cutting through it in Fig. 6.4]. And then Claudia earned three more [continuing to read the problem]. I figured, she probably had 3 dollars before and then she earned three more. So I put the three down there and the three down there [pointing to Fig. 6.4 and to the two threes on the lower half of the pie chart]. But if you go like this, that's a half and that's a half [pointing to each of the halves in the pie chart in Fig. 6.4], so she has a half and she needs a half, so the book costs 12 dollars.

Although we were not able to follow Sara while she was solving the problem, she was able to verbalize, in considerable detail, the process she went through and how she used the notations to solve the problem, similarly to what happened to Charles, with the interviewer's help, in Study 2 of chapter 3. The notation she made helped her, first, to structure her thinking about the problem. When the problem stated that Claudia had one fourth, then earned 3 more dollars, and finally had one half of the money she needed, Sara used the information in the problem to assume—correctly—that each fourth had to be the same and, therefore, each fourth of the money had to be 3 dollars. The notation that she developed from her inference was based on her thinking about fractions and it also helped to expand it. As was the case in the previous problem, it could constitute a step towards an equation such as $x + 3 = 12/2$, from which a solution could be worked out.

Later that same day, Sara, encouraged by David, made a statement about the use of different types of notations. Working on the Claudia and book about lizards' problem, Sara proposed two different notations for the problem. First, she made the notation she had described for Analúcia in front of the whole class and explained it. Then, she made a second notation, saying, "I have another way that isn't using a pie." The notation that she made (see Fig. 6.5) represented the dollar bills that Claudia would need to buy her book.

When she completed this notation, as the video clip shows, David said to her:

FIG. 6.5.   Sara's second notation in front of the whole class.

David: You know, Sara, I think one of the . . . you do two different draw-
             ings. One is a good drawing if you haven't figured it out yet, and
             another one is a drawing that works if, only if you know, if you've
             already figured it out.

Sara: Yeah, if you've already figured it out this one is good [pointing to
             Fig. 6.5], but if you haven't, the pie one would probably be better
             [see Fig. 6.4]. If like someone already did the pie and you want to
             show it differently, you might want to use this one [pointing to
             Fig. 6.5].

It's noteworthy that none of Sara's representations are similar to
Eliza's, for none of them represent all the *actions* described in the problem. As Sara explained, one of these notations, namely, the pie chart
helped her to think about the problem, whereas the other, the currency representation, just showed what she did after solving the problem. However,
we might argue that although the pie chart notation helped her to structure
her thinking, she then also used it to restructure it through her use of dollar
bills in Fig. 6.5: she reorganized the amounts $(3 + 3 = 5 + 1$; and $12 = 10 +
1 + 1)$ into relationships referred to what Claudia had, what Claudia
needed, and the total cost of the book; in addition, she reorganized the
amounts from 1 dollar and 5 dollars to 10 dollars, 1 dollar, and 1 dollar.

SARA EXPLAINS HER USE
OF NOTATIONS TO SOLVE PROBLEMS

In June, after 15 classroom meetings, we interviewed pairs of children
who had participated in our early algebra activities. David interviewed
Sara and another girl (Parabdeep) about the fraction problem in Fig. 6.6, a
follow-up of our last class in May. Again, the selected video clips from
this interview show, more clearly than the transcript below, her use of
written notation to solve problems.

Two-thirds of a fish weighs 10 pounds.
How heavy is the whole fish?

FIG. 6.6.   Problem presented to Sara and Parabdeep during an interview.

Immediately after reading the problem, Sara proposed a solution to it:

Sara: Twenty pounds. Because, two thirds . . . no, wait, fifteen pounds. Cause it would be like [drawing Fig. 6.7] five, ten, fifteen [pointing to each one of the thirds].

David: My goodness.

Sara: And there's ten [pointing to two of the thirds], and there's five [pointing to the 3rd third].

David: So what is the . . . you drew this drawing so quickly! [To Parabdeep:] Parabdeep, she didn't even give us a chance to think about it, did she? Sara, what does this mean? . . . Let's read that again. Two thirds of a fish weighs 10 pounds.

Sara: I thought, I was trying to, because at first I thought it was like that [like fourths—drawing Fig. 6.8] but then I remembered that it was this [like thirds—referring to Fig. 6.7]. So I figured it can't be that [fourths—Fig. 6.5], it had to be this [thirds—Fig. 6.7].

David: Was that in thirds over here before that you drew? [Referring to Fig. 6.8.]

Sara: That was in fourths. I thought, I'm like "two" [referring to the mention of "two thirds" in the problem], and I jumped and I thought it was four.

David: So now you did it this way? [In thirds—referring to Fig. 6.7.]

Sara: Yeah.

FIG. 6.7.   Sara's notation for the fish fraction problem.

FIG. 6.8.   Sara's notation for fourths.

FIG. 6.9.   A "right" notation for thirds.

David: And actually you changed very quickly. And should . . . are these pieces the same size, or are they different sizes? [Referring to the thirds in Fig. 6.7.]

Sara: Well, I don't, when I draw this it's just to help me think of something, so it doesn't really matter.

David: It doesn't really matter. But if you drew it perfectly, should you draw them the same size or different sizes? Or doesn't it matter?

Sara: The same size.

David: Oh, OK.

Sara: So, if I wanted to draw it right, it would probably look like, maybe like that [drawing Fig. 6.9].

Here, Sara is clearly stating that she is using the notation to help her think. The notation is helping her go through the problem and is helpful in allowing her to reflect about the problem. Even the notation that she has not yet made, but is still thinking about, helps her to reflect about the problem.

DISCUSSION

In each of the episodes we analyzed, the notation comes to be a sort of "mental image" (Piaget & Inhelder, 1971) for Sara's understanding of the problem. Objectifying and reifying this mental image (Piaget, 1976; Piaget & García, 1982), she was able to reflect on it, to clarify and further her thinking about the problems. Furthermore, a representation that was initially external and presented as a convention by her teacher in class was subsequently internalized and transformed into a mental representation (see Goldin, 1998; Goldin & Shteingold, 2001; Martí & Pozo, 2000).

Like Cobb's students using the hundreds board (Cobb, 1995), we cannot argue that Sara understood the fraction problems because she had access to the "pie chart" notation. The evidence, furthermore, is not conclusive. For example, we do not have evidence for how her thinking about fractions and her notations for them evolved. What we do have is a small snapshot into the process she went through in solving a series of problems about fractions, and hypotheses about the role that the notations might have played. In addition, we can also say that her notations helped her to reflect on the problems and to further her understanding of the problem. Although the notations could at some point be a reflection of her thinking, they could also be objectified, that is, they could become an object to reflect about the problems even further (see Piaget, 1976; Piaget & García, 1982). The notations Sara made helped her to think about the problems, and in that thinking—and reflecting—process, her understanding about fractions may have further developed.

Sara's initial challenge was to find a notation that would adequately help her to think about the problems at hand. As she herself explained, the pie chart helped her to think about the book of lizards' problems, whereas the dollar bill representation (not one of the "tools" that had been presented to her in class) did not (see Figs. 6.4 and 6.5). Similarly to Babbage's reflection (see Cajori, 1993) about the advantages of algebraic notation, Sara's reasoning was facilitated by the pie charts she made—diagrams that did not, however, describe in detail all that happened in the problem. By compressing meaning into her notations, Sara was able to reason about the problem, using the notation itself as a springboard and a tool for developing that reasoning.

Furthermore, we would venture to argue that Sara's notations supported and furthered her algebraic reasoning. Her notations represented general relations among quantities. As such, they could become the foundation for the development of algebraic equations, as in the case of the line-segment diagrams proposed by Bodanskii (1991) and by Simon and Stimpson (1988). In fact, the notations she made for the ice cream problem (see Fig. 6.2), for the book about lizards problem (see Fig. 6.4), and for the fish weight problem (see Fig. 6.7) could actually stand for any other problem referring to the same quantities. The notations do not express the actions that took place in the problem, or the operations that were carried out with the quantities, but the general relations among the quantities in the problem. The notations she made helped her to change her thinking, and to reflect on the problems presented to her.

Referring back to Kaput's (1991) question "How do material notations and mental constructions interact to produce new constructions?" (p. 55), we could begin by saying that although Sara's notations are not conventional algebraic notations, they do constitute an internalization of a conventional notation accepted within the context of her class. The gradual appropriation of that notation allows her to support and further her algebraic reasoning. That is, we take a midpoint between the dichotomous views presented at the outset of this chapter by Cobb (1995)—the *sociocultural* and the *constructivist* views.

7

Discussion

The findings described in this book suggest that elementary school children can reason algebraically. The interview studies in chapters 2 and 3 show that even 7-year-olds understand that if equals are added or subtracted to equals, the "equation" still holds. Whether they use this principle, however, depends on how problems are presented. Interestingly, verbal problems elicited more logical and transformational justifications than problems with concrete counters, objects on a scale, or equations. Computational justifications or justifications that would focus on the final result of transformations were more often elicited by problems with concrete counters, objects on a scale, or equations. We also found that if all numerical values are given, children overwhelmingly choose to perform computations to determine whether the equality will remain. When not all values were known, however, they would more easily focus on transformations and on the logical principle underlying the situation.

Although many children seemed to search for arithmetical solutions, they were also able to solve the problems taking into account the basic logic underlying the problem situation. We believe that traditional mathematics instruction may be responsible for children's overreliance on a strictly computational approach to problems involving numbers.

Our interviews with U.S. children (chap. 3) replicated the findings with Brazilian children and, further, showed that third graders can develop consistent notations to represent the elements and the relationships in problems involving known and unknown quantities. We found that children intuitively use iconic representations, circles, and shapes to represent unknown amounts and, with some help, they can use a canceling-out strategy to eliminate equal unknown amounts that appear on both sides of the equality they are dealing with, thus simplifying the equation and finding the problem's solution. This foreshadows the syntactic rules of algebra for dealing with unknown quantities that appear on both sides of equations.

In chapters 4, 5, and 6 we found that, when asked to consider function tables and variables, the children initially made use of nonalgebraic approaches and solutions. However, with practice and participation in the Early Algebra activities we designed, they shifted towards general properties of numerical relations and functions.

In our classroom observations, we found that children use mathematical notations not only to register what they understood, but also to structure and help further their thinking, allowing them to make inferences they might otherwise not have made.

The results of our intervention open up new possibilities for the teaching of an algebrafied arithmetic, but leave us with many other issues to be dealt with and questions to be answered. These questions relate to three central issues in mathematics education, namely, the development versus learning debate, the role of contexts and situations in mathematical learning, and the role of representational systems in mathematics understanding. Let's consider each of these:

DEVELOPMENT VERSUS LEARNING

Several years ago, prominent researchers posited the existence of a "cognitive gap" between arithmetic and algebra in an attempt to explain why many adolescents had trouble learning algebra (see our review in chap. 1). Underlying their thinking was an assumption about "developmental readiness": Many adolescents were presumably not developmentally ready to learn algebra. As evidence began to fall on the side of those defending the notion that young students *can* learn algebra, the developmentalist position has lost ground. Our findings showing that, given the appropriate conditions, young students can learn to reason algebraically, further undermine this extreme developmentalist position.[14] It now seems that the students' difficulties identified in prior research stem in part from limitations in teaching and curriculum design. As others have pointed out before (Booth, 1988; Kaput, 1998; Schoenfeld, 1995), the traditional mathematics curricula, with an overbearing emphasis on the computational aspects of arithmetic, may have exacerbated the difficulties that children face when learning algebra.

But development obviously also plays a major role in the development of mathematical reasoning: Our research has helped identify concepts that require a long time to mature. In more recent work, for example, we found that the idea of "difference," fundamental to the students' understanding of additive structures, takes a long time to evolve. It follows directly from the fact that integers comprise a group that any pair of them, a, b, will have a unique difference, $a - b$. This idea takes on subtle differences in meaning across the contexts of number lines, measurement, subtraction, tables, graphs and vector diagrams (Carraher, Brizuela, & Earnest, 2001).

As we discussed elsewhere (Schliemann & Carraher, 2002), mathematical understanding is an individual construction that is transformed and expanded through social interaction and access to cultural systems and cultural tools. The teaching and learning of algebra should unfold from children's basic understandings, leading to more general, complex, and explicit knowledge. To achieve this, we need to provide children with instructional activities that can further expand their initial understandings and representation tools.

CONTEXTS

Professional mathematicians generally do not investigate contexts. Yet contexts are crucial to mathematics educators' concerns because students, particularly young students, learn mathematics through reasoning about various types of situations and activities: buying and selling, making sense

---

[14]This, however, hasn't convinced the authors of the "cognitive gap" notion, who claim that students only are engaging in algebra if they can understand and use the syntax of algebra and solve equations with variables on each side of the equals sign (see Filloy & Rojano, 1989). Most researchers, ourselves included, regard this criterion for distinguishing between algebra and non-algebra as too narrow.

of data, measurement, astronomy, population growth, and so on. A wide range of important research aims to determine how reasoning about situations can foster mathematical understanding (see Moshkovich & Brenner, 2002, for examples of studies in this area, including our review chapter, Carraher & Schliemann, 2002a).

The main challenge contexts pose concerns how abstract knowledge about mathematical objects and structures come out of experience and reasoning in particular situations. History offers approaches ranging from Platonism (that attributes mathematical knowledge to reminiscence and thus minimizes the role of experience), through Piagetian structuralism (whereby internalized actions constitute schemes that form the basis of logical and mathematical operations), to situated cognition (that denies that knowledge ever becomes independent of thinking about situations).

In our early research about mathematical thinking in out of school contexts (Carraher, Carraher, & Schliemann, 1985, 1987; Nunes, Schliemann, & Carraher, 1993), we provided detailed examples of how work contexts (commerce, carpentry, etc.) engender mathematical understanding and influence the forms it takes; in this early work we sometimes referred to simple computation problems as being "context-free." We later began to document (Schliemann, 1995; Schliemann, Araujo, Cassundé, Macedo, & Nicéas, 1998) how contexts sometimes help and, at other times hinder, mathematical reasoning. More recently (e.g., Carraher & Schliemann, 2002a; Schliemann & Carraher, 2002) we have begun to compare and contrast *everyday contexts* with *mathematical contexts*.

Although contextualized problems and focus on quantities help in providing meaning for mathematical relations and structures, we must recognize that algebraic knowledge cannot be fully grounded in thinking about quantities. This however, should not prevent young children to learn algebra. In fact, our work with third-grade students shows that they can work, and do enjoy working with pure numerical relations unassociated with particular contexts or physical quantities.

This does not mean that situational contexts are mere distractions to mathematical problems (Carraher & Schliemann, 2002a, b, and Schliemann & Carraher, 2002). Much of the power and meaning of mathematics comes from our ability to apply it to a wide range of situations. This can only be achieved by working out the way in which mathematical concepts and representational tools relate to the particular characteristics of the situations. We must be careful not to dismiss the considerable effort students must make in such adaptations. Important questions for Early Algebra research underlie the tension between contextualized situations and mathematical structures and relations.

THE ROLES OF REPRESENTATIONAL SYSTEMS IN MATHEMATICAL LEARNING

Mathematics employs symbols to stand for mathematical objects and ideas that are not, themselves, physical things: numerals to represent numbers, letters to stand for variables, specialized characters such as $\times$, $\sum$, $\leq$, and $\forall$ to stand for mathematical and logical operations. These symbols are integral components of *symbolic* or *representational systems* that possess a syntactical structure. The basic representational systems of mathematics are *algebraic-symbolic notation*, *natural language*, *numerical expressions* (including number sentences and data/function tables), and *geometrical displays* (e.g., number lines and graphs).

In a narrow sense, algebraic reasoning concerns only algebraic symbolic notation. In the broad sense used here, algebraic reasoning is associated with and embedded in each of the above representational systems.[15] Much of the work in learning to think algebraically consists in learning how to generate representations in one system from representations given in another (Bamberger, 1990). Schwartz and Yerushalmy (1992b, 1995) and Goldin (1998) have highlighted the importance of building relationships among different representations. Recently, the National Council of Teachers of Mathematics (NCTM, 2000) has acknowledged the importance of "translating" or establishing relationships among multiple modes of representation. Representations have been recognized as one of the process standards, meant to highlight ways of acquiring and using content knowledge in the area of mathematics. NCTM states that, "different representations often illuminate different aspects of a complex concept or relationship. Thus, in order to become deeply knowledgeable about [a specific mathematical concept]—and many other concepts in school mathemat-

---

[15]This does not mean that all mathematical representations express mathematical reasoning. It is necessary that the user articulate a general idea that is amenable to expression through algebraic-symbolic notation.

ics—students will need a variety of representations that support their understanding" (p. 68).

Cross-representational activity is thus fundamental to the task of producing a research basis in Early Algebra. Early Algebra research needs to look more closely at how students establish correspondences across various representations.

A number of important questions concern the role of algebraic representations, narrowly defined: Should formal algebraic notation be a part of Early Algebra activities? Under what circumstances is it useful (or not) to introduce algebraic notation? Should algebraic notation be semantically or syntactically driven?

Although some educators argue against any and all uses of algebraic-symbolic notation in the early grades, we feel it is better to frame the issue in a broad context and then answer it on the basis of research. By "broad context," we mean to ask more generally how notations[16] relate to mathematical reasoning. Then we can assess the particular case of algebraic-symbolic notation.

FUTURE DEVELOPMENTS

We suggest that the evidence we presented be assessed in terms of the extent that it demonstrates that students are engaging in meaningful, productive discussions about functions. At a future point, we would hope to return to these same issues with a summative evaluation of learning. But at this moment, the claim is not that a great deal has been learned or that a particular teaching technique "works." We claim merely that some mathematical ideas critical to reforming the early mathematics education are within reach of students.

We showed the potential of Early Algebra activities in expanding students' mathematical reasoning and in helping them develop and use algebra notations and tools to solve problems. But we did not explore the limits of children's capabilities regarding algebra. In fact, we may have underestimated children's potential to learn algebra.

---

[16]We use "notations" to include any external symbolic representations, not merely algebraic script.

The issue of sustainability of learning is also still open. In our classroom research we met with the students only a few times per school term. A year after we had ended our teaching intervention in their classroom, when in 4th grade (May, 2000), the children who participated in our classroom activities took the Massachusetts Comprehensive Assessment System (MCAS), a high-stake standardized state mandated test. We were pleasantly surprised to see that, even though we were not focusing on typical MCAS questions, the children who worked with us performed significantly better than their peers from the other non-participating classrooms in the same school ($t = 2.53$, $p = .0128$). We believe, and this is what we want to test in new studies, that much more can be achieved if children participate in early algebra activities on a daily basis.

We still need to document how students learn to overlook certain everyday considerations or make assumptions about ideal conditions so that the everyday context can map conveniently onto the mathematics relations. Totally ignoring real-world constraints has its drawbacks, as realistic mathematics supporters have noted (Verschaffel, Greer, & DeCorte, 2002). We propose to make idealized assumptions about reality explicit in our future instruction, to highlight the tension between everyday and academic mathematics.

In future research, we also hope to explore appropriate scenarios for facilitating an understanding of variables and functions beyond particular instantiations. Through close descriptions such as those provided in this book, we hope to help the mathematics education community of researchers and practitioners uncover the true potential behind an early introduction of algebraic concepts and notations.

Finally, we also need to investigate how algebraic notation becomes instrumental to mathematical reasoning. In part this concerns how it becomes syntactically driven. Because it remains important for students to be able to interpret algebraic-symbolic expressions with respect to rich contexts, semantic meaning is never to be fully abandoned. And one of the challenges for our research is to show how each sort of reasoning emerges and relates to the other.

References

Ainley, J. (1999). Doing algebra-type stuff: Emergent algebra in the primary school. In O. Zaslavsky (Ed.), *Proceedings of the Twenty Third Annual Conference of the International Group for the Psychology of Mathematics Education* (Vol. 2, pp. 9–16). Haifa, Israel.

Bamberger, J. (1990). The laboratory for making things: Developing multiple representations of knowledge. In D. A. Schön (Ed.), *The reflective turn* (pp. 37–62). New York: Teachers College Press.

Bednarz, N. (2001). A problem-solving approach to algebra: Accounting for the reasonings and notations developed by students. In H. Chick, K. Stacey, J. Vincent, & J. Vincent (Eds.), *The future of the teaching and learning of algebra: Proceedings of the 12th ICMI Study Conference* (Vol. 1, pp. 69–78). Melbourne, Australia: The University of Melbourne.

Bednarz, N., & Janvier, B. (1996). Emergence and development of algebra as a problem solving tool: Continuities and discontinuities with arithmetic. In N. Bednarz, C. Kieran, & L. Lee (Eds.), *Approaches to algebra. Perspectives for research and teaching* (pp. 115–136). Dordrecht, The Netherlands: Kluwer.

Bellisio, C., & Maher, C. (1998). What kind of notation do children use to express algebraic thinking? In S. Berenson, K. Dawkins, M. Blanton, W. Coulombe, J. Kolb, K. Norwood, & L. Stiffet (Eds.), *Proceedings of the XX Annual Meeting of the North American Chapter of the International Group for the Psychology of Mathematics Education* (pp. 161–165). Raleigh, NC.

Blanton, M., & Kaput, J. (2000). Generalizing and progressively formalizing in a third grade mathematics classroom: Conversations about even and odd numbers. In M. Fernández (Ed.), *Proceedings of the XXII Annual Meeting of the North American Chapter of the International Group for the Psychology of Mathematics Education* (p. 115), Columbus, OH: ERIC Clearinghouse.

127

Bodanskii, F. (1991). The formation of an algebraic method of problem solving in primary school children. In V. Davydov (Ed.), *Soviet studies in mathematics education. Psychological abilities of primary school children in learning mathematics* (Vol. 6, pp. 275–338). Reston, VA: The National Council of Teachers of Mathematics.

Booth, L. (1984). *Algebra: Children's strategies and errors.* Windsor, UK: NFER-Nelson.

Booth, L. (1987). Equations revisited. In J. Bergeron, N. Herscovics, & C. Kieran (Eds.), *Proceedings: XI International Conference Psychology of Mathematics Education* (Vol. I, pp. 282–288). Montreal, Canada.

Booth, L. R. (1988). Children's difficulties in beginning algebra. In A. F. Coxford & A. P. Shulte (Eds.), *The ideas of algebra, K–12: 1988 Yearbook* (pp. 20–32). Reston, VA: The National Council of Teachers of Mathematics.

Boulton-Lewis, G. M., Cooper, T. J., Atweh, B., Pillay, H., & Wilss, L. (2001). Readiness for algebra. In T. Nakahara & M. Koyama (Eds.), *Proceedings of the XXIV International Conference for the Psychology of Mathematics Education* (Vol. 2, pp. 89–96). Hiroshima, Japan.

Brito-Lima, A. P. (1996). *Desenvolvimento da representação de igualdades em crianças de primeira a sexta série do primeiro grau* [The development of the representation of equalities among first to sixth graders]. Unpublished master's thesis. Mestrado em Psicologia, Universidade Federal de Pernambuco, Recife, Brazil.

Brito-Lima, A. P., & da Rocha Falcão, J. T. (1997). Early development of algebraic representation among 6–13 year-old children: The importance of didactic contract. In E. Pehkonen (Ed.), *Proceedings of the XXI International Conference Psychology of Mathematics Education* (Vol. 2, pp. 201–208). Lahti, Finland.

Brizuela, B. M. (2004). *Mathematical development in young children: Exploring notations.* New York: Teachers College Press.

Cajori, F. (1993). *A history of mathematical notations, vol. 2: Notations mainly in higher mathematics.* Chicago, IL: The Open Court Publishing Company. (Original work published 1929)

Carpenter, T., & Franke, M. (2001). Developing algebraic reasoning in the elementary school: Generalization and proof. In H. Chick, K. Stacey, J. Vincent, & J. Vincent (Eds.), *The future of the teaching and learning of algebra. Proceedings of the 12th ICMI Study Conference* (Vol. 1, pp. 155–162). Melbourne, Australia: The University of Melbourne.

Carpenter, T., & Levi, L. (2000). *Developing conceptions of algebraic reasoning in the primary grades* (Research Report 00-2). Madison, WI: National Center for Improving Student Learning and Achievement in Mathematics and Science. Article available at http://www.wcer.wisc.edu/ncisl

Carraher, D. W., Brizuela, B. M., & Earnest, D. (2001). The reification of additive differences in early algebra. In H. Chick, K. Stacey, J. Vincent, & J. Vincent (Eds.), *The future of the teaching and learning of algebra. Proceedings of the 12th ICMI Study Conference* (Vol. 1, pp. 163–170). Melbourne, Australia: The University of Melbourne.

Carraher, D. W., Nemirovsky, R., & DiMattia, C. (Eds.). (in press). Media and meaning. CD-ROM issue of *Monographs of the Journal for Research in Mathematics Education.*

Carraher, D. W., & Schliemann, A. D. (2002a). Is everyday mathematics truly relevant to mathematics education? In J. Moshkovich & M. Brenner (Eds.), *Everyday mathematics. Monographs of the Journal for Research in Mathematics Education* (pp. 131–153). Reston, VA: The National Council of Teachers of Mathematics.

Carraher, D. W., & Schliemann, A. D. (2002b). Modeling reasoning. In K. Gravemeijer, R. Lehrer, B. Oers, & L. Verschaffel (Eds.), *Symbolizing, modeling and tool use in mathematics education* (pp. 295–304). The Netherlands: Kluwer.

Carraher, D. W., Schliemann, A., & Brizuela, B. (1999, April). *Bringing out the algebraic character of arithmetic.* Paper presented at the 1999 AERA Meeting, Montreal, Canada. Available at http://www.earlyalgebra.terc.edu

Carraher, D. W., Schliemann, A. D., & Brizuela, B. (2000). *Early algebra, early arithmetic: Treating operations as functions.* Plenary address presented at the Twenty-second Annual Meeting of the North American Chapter of the International Group for the Psychology of Mathematics Education, Tucson, Arizona.

Carraher, T. N., Carraher, D. W., & Schliemann, A. D. (1985). Mathematics in the streets and in schools. *British Journal of Developmental Psychology, 3,* 21–29.

Carraher, T. N., Carraher, D. W., & Schliemann, A. D. (1987). Written and oral mathematics. *Journal for Research in Mathematics Education, 18,* 83–97.

Carraher, T. N., & Schliemann, A. D. (1987). Manipulating equivalences in the market and in maths. In J. Bergeron, N. Herscovics, & C. Kieran (Eds.), *Proceedings: XI International Conference Psychology Mathematics Education* (Vol. I, pp. 289–294). Montreal, Canada.

Ceci, S. J. (1990). *On intelligence . . . more or less: A bio-ecological treatise on intellectual development.* Englewood Cliffs, NJ: Prentice Hall.

Ceci, S. J. (1993). Some contextual trends in cognitive development. *Developmental Review, 13,* 403–435.

Ceci, S. J., & Bronfenbrenner, U. (1985). Don't forget to take the cupcakes out of the oven: Strategic time-monitoring, prospective memory and context. *Child Development, 56,* 175–190.

Chazan, D. (1993). High school geometry students' justifications for their views of empirical evidence and mathematical proof. *Educational Studies in Mathematics, 24,* 359–387.

Chick, K., Stacey, J., Vincent, J., & Vincent, J. (Eds.). (2001). *The future of the teaching and learning of algebra: Proceedings of the 12th ICMI Study Conference.* Melbourne, Australia: The University of Melbourne.

Cobb, P. (1995). Cultural tools and mathematical learning: A case study. *Journal for Research in Mathematics Education, 26,* 62–385.

Collis, K. (1975). *The development of formal reasoning.* Newcastle, Australia: University of Newcastle.

Cortes, A., Kavafian, N., & Vergnaud, G. (1990). From arithmetic to algebra: Negotiating a jump in the learning process. In G. Booker, P. Cobb, & T. De Mendicuti (Eds.), *Proceedings of the XIV International Conference Psychology of Mathematics Education* (Vol. II, pp. 27–34). Oaxtepec, Mexico.

Crawford, A. R. (2001). Developing algebraic thinking: Past, present, and future. In H. Chick, K. Stacey, J. Vincent, & J. Vincent (Eds.), *The future of the teaching and learning of algebra: Proceedings of the 12th ICMI Study Conference* (Vol. 1, pp. 192–198). Melbourne, Australia: The University of Melbourne.

Da Rocha Falcão, J. (1993). A álgebra como ferramenta de representação e resolução de problemas [Algebra as a tool to represent and solve problems]. In A. Schliemann, D. Carraher, A. Spinillo, L. Meira, & J. Falcão (Eds.), *Estudos em psicologia da educação matemática* (pp. 85–107). Recife, Brazil: Editora Universitária UFPE.

Da Rocha Falcão, J. T., Brito Lima, A. P., Araújo, C. R., Lins Lessa, M. M., & Osório, M. O. (2000). A didactic sequence for the introduction of algebraic activity in early elementary school. In T. Nakahara & M. Koyama (Eds.), *Proceedings of the XXIV Conference of the International group for the Psychology of Mathematics Education* (Vol. 2, pp. 209–216). Hiroshima, Japan.

Davis, R. (1967). *Exploration in mathematics. A text for teachers.* Palo Alto, CA: Addison-Wesley.

Davis, R. (1971–1972). Observing children's mathematical behavior as a foundation for curriculum planning. *The Journal of Children's Mathematical Behavior, 1*(1), 7–59.

Davis, R. (1985). ICME-5 Report: Algebraic thinking in the early grades. *Journal of Mathematical Behavior, 4,* 195–208.

Davis, R. (1989). Theoretical considerations: Research studies in how humans think about algebra. In S. Wagner & C. Kieran (Eds.), *Research issues in the learning and teaching of algebra* (Vol. 4, pp. 266–274). Reston, VA: The National Council of Teachers of Mathematics/Lawrence Erlbaum Associates.

Davydov, V. (Ed.). (1991). *Soviet studies in mathematics education, vol. 6: Psychological abilities of primary school children in learning mathematics.* Reston, VA: The National Council of Teachers of Mathematics. (Original work published 1969)

Demana, F., & Leitzel, J. (1988). Establishing fundamental concepts through numerical problem solving. In A. Coxford & A. Shulte (Eds.), *The ideas of algebra, K–12: 1988 Yearbook* (pp. 61–69). Reston, VA: The National Council of Teachers of Mathematics.

Dias, M. G., & Harris, P. L. (1988). The effect of make-believe play on deductive reasoning. *British Journal of Developmental Psychology, 6,* 207–221.

Donaldson, M. (1978). *Children's minds.* Glasgow, UK: Fontana/Collins.

Euclid. (1956). Book V. Propositions I–VII [Related to Eudoxus' theory of proportion]. In T. L. Heath (Ed.), *The thirteen books of Euclid's Elements* (Part II, pp. 138–148). New York: Dover Publications.

Filloy, E., & Rojano, T. (1984). From an arithmetical to an algebraic thought. In *Proceedings: VI Annual Meeting of PME, North American Chapter.* Montreal, Canada.

Filloy, E., & Rojano, T. (1989). Solving equations: The transition from arithmetic to algebra. *For the Learning of Mathematics, 9*(2), 19–25.

Fishbein, E., & Keden, I. (1982). Proof and certitude in the development of mathematical thinking. In A. Vermandel (Ed.), *Proceedings of the Sixth International Conference for the Psychology of Mathematics Education* (pp. 128–131). Antwerp, Belgium: Universitatire Instelling Antwerpen.

Freudenthal, H. (1983). *Didactical phenomenology of mathematical structures.* Dordrecht, The Netherlands: Reidel.

Fridman, L. M. (1991). Features of introducing the concept of concrete numbers in the primary grades. In V. Davydov (Ed.), *Soviet studies in mathematics education, Vol. 6: Psychological abilities of primary school children in learning mathematics* (pp. 148–180). Reston, VA: The National Council of Teachers of Mathematics. (Original work published 1969)

Fujii, T., & Stephens, M. (2001). Fostering an understanding of algebraic generalization through numerical expressions: The role of quasi-variable. In H. Chick, K. Stacey, J. Vincent, & J. Vincent (Eds.), *The future of the teaching and learning of algebra: Proceedings of the 12th ICMI Study Conference* (Vol. 1, pp. 258–264). Melbourne, Australia: The University of Melbourne.

Goldin, G. (1998). Representational systems, learning, and problem solving in mathematics. *Journal of Mathematical Behavior, 17*(2), 137–165.

Goldin, G., & Shteingold, N. (2001). Systems of representations and the development of mathematical concepts. In A. A. Cuoco & F. R. Curcio (Eds.), *The roles of representation in school mathematics. The National Council of Teachers of Mathematics 2001 Yearbook* (pp. 1–23). Reston, VA: The National Council of Teachers of Mathematics.

Greer, B. (1994). Extending the meaning of multiplication and division. In G. Harel & J. Confrey (Eds.), *The development of multiplicative reasoning in the learning of mathematics* (pp. 61–88). Albany, NY: State University of New York Press.

Harper, E. (1987). Ghosts of Diophantus. *Educational Studies in Mathematics, 18*, 75–90.

Hatano, G. (1982). Cognitive consequences of practice on culture specific skills. *Quarterly Newsletter of the Laboratory of Comparative Human Cognition, 4*, 15–18.

Healy, L., Hoyles, C., & Sutherland, R. (1990). Critical decisions in the generalization process: A methodology for researching pupil collaboration in computer and non-computer environments. In G. Booker, P. Cobb, & T. De Mendicuti (Eds.), *Proceedings of the Fourteenth PME Conference* (Vol. III, pp. 83–90). Oaxtepec, Mexico.

Heath, T. L. (1956). (Ed.). *The thirteen books of Euclid's Elements.* New York: Dover Publications.

Heid, M. K. (1996). A technology-intensive functional approach to the emergence of algebraic thinking. In N. Bednarz, C. Kieran, & L. Lee (Eds.), *Approaches to algebra: Perspectives for research and teaching* (pp. 239–255). Dordrecht, The Netherlands: Kluwer.

Herscovics, N., & Kieran, C. (1980, November). Constructing meaning for the concept of equation. *Mathematics Teacher*, 572–580.

Herscovics, N., & Linchevski, L. (1994). A cognitive gap between arithmetic and algebra. *Educational Studies in Mathematics, 27*, 59–78.

Hoyles, C., & Noss, R. (1987). Children working in a structured learning environment: From doing to understanding. *Recherche en Didactique des Mathematiques, 8*(1,2), 131–174.

Hoyles, C., & Noss, R. (Eds.). (1992). *Learning mathematics and logo.* Cambridge, MA: MIT Press.

Hume, D. (1737–1740/2003). *A treatise of human nature.* Mineola, NY: Dover Publications.

Kaput, J. (1991). Notations and representations as mediators of constructive processes. In E. von Glasersfeld (Ed.), *Radical constructivism in mathematics education* (pp. 53–74). Dordrecht, The Netherlands: Kluwer.

Kaput, J. (1998). Transforming algebra from an engine of inequity to an engine of mathematical power by "algebrafying" the K–12 curriculum. In National Council of Teachers of Mathematics (Eds.), *The nature and role of algebra in the K–14 curriculum*. Washington, DC: National Academy Press.

Kaput, J., & Blanton, M. (2001). Algebrafying the elementary mathematics experience. Part I: Transforming task structures. In H. Chick, K. Stacey, J. Vincent, & J. Vincent (Eds.), *The future of the teaching and learning of algebra: Proceedings of the 12th ICMI Study Conference* (Vol. 1, pp. 344–350). Melbourne, Australia: The University of Melbourne.

Kaput, J., & West, M. (1994). Missing value proportional reasoning problems: Factors affecting informal reasoning patterns. In G. Harel & J. Confrey (Eds.), *The development of multiplicative reasoning in the learning of mathematics* (pp. 237–287). Albany, NY: State University of New York Press.

Kieran, C. (1981). Concepts associated with the equality symbol. *Educational Studies in Mathematics, 12*, 317–326.

Kieran, C. (1985). The equation-solving errors of novices and intermediate algebra students. In *Proceedings: IX International Conference Psychology of Mathematics Education*. Montreal.

Kieran, C. (1989). The early learning of algebra: A structural perspective. In S. Wagner & C. Kieran (Eds.), *Research issues in the learning and teaching of algebra* (Vol. 4, pp. 33–56). Reston, VA: The National Council of Teachers of Mathematics/Lawrence Erlbaum Associates.

Kieran, C., Boileau, A., & Garançon, A. (1996). Introducing algebra by means of a technology-supported, functional approach. In N. Bednarz, C. Kieran, & L. Lee (Eds.), *Approaches to algebra: Perspectives for research and teaching* (pp. 257–293). Dordrecht, The Netherlands: Kluwer.

Kuchemann, D. E. (1981). Algebra. In K. Hart (Ed.), *Children's understanding of mathematics* (pp. 102–119). London: Murray.

Laborde, C. (1982). *Langue naturelle et écriture symbolique: deux codes en interaction dans l'enseignement mathématique* [Natural language and written symbols: two codes in interaction in mathematics teaching]. Unpublished doctoral dissertation, Université Scientifique et Médicale, Grenoble, France.

LaCampagne, C. B. (1995). *The algebra initiative colloquium. Vol. 2: Working group papers*. Washington, DC: U.S. Department of Education, OERI.

Lee, L., & Wheeler, D. (1989). The arithmetic connection. *Educational Studies in Mathematics, 20*, 41–54.

Light, P., Buckingham, N., & Robbins, A. (1979). The conservation task as an interactional setting. *British Journal of Educational Psychology, 49*, 304–310.

Lins Lessa, M. M. (1995). A balança de dois pratos versus problemas verbais na iniciação à algebra [Two-pan scale versus verbal problems in introductory algebra]. Unpublished master's thesis, Mestrado em Psicologia, Universidade Federal de Pernambuco, Recife, Brazil.

MacGregor, M. (1996). Curricular aspects of arithmetic and algebra. In J. Gimenez, R. C. Lins, & B. Gomez (Eds.), *Arithmetics and algebra education: Searching for the future* (pp. 50–54). Tarragona, Spain: Universitat Rovira i Virgili.

MacGregor, M. (2001). Does learning algebra benefit most people? In H. Chick, K. Stacey, J. Vincent, & J. Vincent (Eds.), *The future of the teaching and learning of algebra: Proceedings of the 12th ICMI Study Conference* (Vol. 2, pp. 405–411). Melbourne, Australia: The University of Melbourne.

Martí, E., & Pozo, J. I. (2000). Más allá de las representaciones mentales: la adquisición de los sistemas externos de representación [Beyond mental representations: the acquisition of external representation systems]. *Infancia y Aprendizaje, 90*, 11–30.

Mason, J. (1996). Expressing generality and roots of algebra. In N. Bednarz, C. Kieran, & L. Lee (Eds.), *Approaches to algebra* (pp. 65–86). Dordrecht, The Netherlands: Kluwer.

McGarrigle, J., & Donaldson, M. (1974). Conservation accidents. *Cognition, 3*, 341–350.

Morris, A. (1995). *Development of algebraic reasoning in children and adolescents: Cultural, curricular, and age-related effects.* Unpublished doctoral dissertation, Ohio State University.

Moshkovich, J., & Brenner, M. (Eds.). (2002). *Everyday mathematics. Monographs of the Journal for Research in Mathematics Education.* Reston, VA: The National Council of Teachers of Mathematics.

National Council of Teachers of Mathematics. (1989). *Curriculum and evaluation standards for school mathematics.* Reston, VA: Author.

National Council of Teachers of Mathematics. (1997). *A framework for constructing a vision of algebra. Algebra working group document.* Reston, VA: Author.

National Council of Teachers of Mathematics. (2000). *Principles and standards for school mathematics.* Reston, VA: Author.

Nemirovsky, R. (1994). On ways of symbolizing: The case of Laura and velocity sign. *Journal of Mathematical Behavior, 13*(4), 389–422.

Noss, R. (1986). Constructing a conceptual framework for elementary algebra through Logo programming. *Educational Studies in Mathematics, 17*(4), 335–357.

Nunes, T., Schliemann, A. D., & Carraher, D. W. (1993). *Mathematics in the streets and in schools.* Cambridge, UK: Cambridge University Press.

Papert, S. (1980). *Mindstorms.* New York: Basic Books.

Piaget, J. (1970a). *Science of education and the psychology of the child.* New York: Orion Press.

Piaget, J. (1970b). *The child's conception of movement and speed.* London: Routledge & Kegan Paul. (Original work published 1946)

Piaget, J. (1976). *The grasp of consciousness: Action and concept in the young child* (S. Wedgwood, Trans.). Cambridge, MA: Harvard University Press. (Original work published 1974)

Piaget, J., & García, R. (1982). *Psicogénesis e historia de la ciencia* [Psychogenesis and the history of science]. México: Siglo Veintiuno Editores.

Piaget, J., & Inhelder, B. (1971). *Mental imagery in the child* (P. A. Chilton, Trans.). New York: Basic Books. (Original work published 1966)

Resnick, L. B. (1986). The development of mathematical intuition. In M. Perlmutter (Ed.), *Perspectives on intellectual development: The Minnesota Symposium on Child Psychology* (Vol. 19, pp. 159–194). Hillsdale, NJ: Lawrence Erlbaum Associates.

Resnick, L., Cauzinille-Marmeche, E., & Mathieu, J. (1987). Understanding algebra. In J. Sloboda & D. Rogers (Eds.), *Cognitive processes in mathematics* (pp. 169–203). Oxford, UK: Clarendon Press.

Ricco, G. (1982). Les premières acquisitions de la notion de fonction linéaire chez l'enfant de 7 . . . 11 ans [The first notions of linear functions among 7 to 10 year-olds]. *Educational Studies in Mathematics, 13*, 289–327.

Rojano, T. (1996). Developing algebraic aspects of problem solving within a spreadsheet environment. In N. Bednarz, C. Kieran, & L. Lee (Eds.), *Approaches to algebra* (pp. 137–145). Dordrecht, The Netherlands: Kluwer.

Schifter, D. (1999). Reasoning about operations: Early algebraic thinking, grades K through 6. In L. Stiff & F. Curio (Eds.), *Mathematical reasoning, K–12: 1999 National Council of Teachers of Mathematics yearbook* (pp. 62–81). Reston, VA: The National Council of Teachers of Mathematics.

Schliemann, A. D. (1995). Some concerns about bringing everyday mathematics to mathematics education: Plenary address. In L. Meira & D. Carraher (Eds.), *Proceedings of the XIX International Conference for the Psychology of Mathematics Education* (Vol. 1, pp. 45–60). Recife, Brazil.

Schliemann, A. D. (2000). Constraint, cooperation, and algebraic problem solving. *New Ideas in Psychology, 18*(2–3), 157–169.

Schliemann, A. D., & Acioly, N. M. (1989). Mathematical knowledge developed at work: The contributions of practice versus the contribution of schooling. *Cognition and Instruction, 6*(3), 185–221.

Schliemann, A. D., Araujo, C., Cassundé, M. A., Macedo, S., & Nicéas, L. (1998). Multiplicative commutativity in school children and street sellers. *Journal for Research in Mathematics Education, 29*(4), 422–435.

Schliemann, A., Brito-Lima, A., & Santiago, M. (1992). Understanding equivalences through balance scales. In W. Geeslin & K. Graham (Eds.), *Proceedings: XVI International Conference Psychology of Mathematics Education* (Vol. II, pp. 298–305). Durham, NH.

Schliemann, A. D., & Carraher, D. W. (1992). Proportional reasoning in and out of school. In P. Light & G. Butterworth (Eds.), *Context and cognition* (pp. 47–73). Hemel Hempstead: Harvester-Wheatsheaf.

Schliemann, A. D., & Carraher, D. W. (2002). The evolution of mathematical understanding: Everyday versus idealized reasoning. *Developmental Review, 22*(2), 242–266.

Schliemann, A. D., Carraher, D. W., & Ceci, S. J. (1997). Everyday cognition. In J. W. Berry, P. R. Dasen, & T. S. Sarawathi (Eds.), *Handbook of cross-cultural psychology: Vol. 2. Basic processes and developmental psychology* (2nd ed., pp. 177–215). Boston: Allyn & Bacon.

Schliemann, A. D., & Magalhães, V. P. (1990). Proportional reasoning: From shopping, to kitchens, laboratories, and, hopefully, schools. In G. Booker, P. Cobb, & T. De Mendicuti (Eds.), *Proceedings of the XIV PME conference* (Vol. III, pp. 67–73). Oaxtepec, Mexico.

Schliemann, A. D., & Nunes, T. (1990). A situated schema of proportionality. *British Journal of Developmental Psychology, 8,* 259–268.

Schoenfeld, A. (1995). Report of Working Group 1. In C. B. LaCampagne (Ed.), *The algebra initiative colloquium. Vol. 2: Working group papers* (pp. 11–18). Washington, DC: U.S. Department of Education, OERI.

Schoenfeld, A., & Arcavi, A. (1988). On the meaning of variable. *Mathematics Teacher, 81,* 420–427.

Schwartz, J. (1995). Shuttling between the particular and the general. In D. Perkins, J. Schwartz, West, & S. Wiske (Eds.), *Software goes to school: Teaching for understanding with new technologies* (pp. 93–105). New York: Oxford University Press.

Schwartz, J. (1996). *Semantic aspects of quantity.* Unpublished manuscript. Cambridge, MA: MIT and Harvard Graduate School of Education.

Schwartz, J., & Yerushalmy, M. (1991). *Getting students to function in algebra.* Unpublished manuscript.

Schwartz, J., & Yerushalmy, M. (1992a). *The geometric supposer.* Pleasantville, NY: Sunburst Communications.

Schwartz, J., & Yerushalmy, M. (1992b). *The function supposer; symbols and graphs.* Pleasantville, NY: Sunburst Communications.

Schwartz, J., & Yerushalmy, M. (1995). On the need for a bridging language for mathematical modeling. *For the Learning of Mathematics, 15*(2), 29–35.

Sfard, A. (1995). The development of algebra: Confronting historical and psychological perspectives. *Journal of Mathematical Behavior, 14,* 15–39.

Sfard, A., & Linchevski, L. (1994). The gains and the pitfalls of reification—the case of algebra. *Educational Studies in Mathematics, 26,* 191–228.

Simon, M. A., & Stimpson, V. C. (1988). Developing algebraic representation using diagrams. In A. F. Coxford & A. P. Shulte (Eds.), *The ideas of algebra, K–12* (pp. 136–141). Reston, VA: The National Council of Teachers of Mathematics.

Slavitt, D. (1999). The role of operation sense in transitions from arithmetic to algebraic thought. *Educational Studies in Mathematics, 37,* 251–274.

Smith, S. (2000). Second graders discoveries of algebraic generalizations. In M. Fernández (Ed.), *Proceedings of the XXII Annual Meeting of the North American Chapter of the International Group for the Psychology of Mathematics Education* (pp. 133–139). Columbus, OH: ERIC Clearinghouse.

Steinberg, R., Sleeman, D., & Ktorza, D. (1990). Algebra students knowledge of equivalence of equations. *Journal for Research in Mathematics Education, 22*(2), 112–121.

Sutherland, R. (1989). Providing a computer-based framework for algebraic thinking. *Educational Studies in Mathematics, 20*(3), 317–344.

Sutherland, R. (1993). Symbolizing through spreadsheets. *Micromath, 10*(1), 20–22.

Sutherland, R., & Rojano, T. (1993). A spreadsheet approach to solving algebra problems. *Journal of Mathematical Behavior, 12,* 353–383.

Thompson, P. (1991, April). *Quantitative reasoning, complexity, and additive structures.* Paper presented at the 1991 AERA Meeting, Chicago, IL.

Thompson, P. (1994). The development of the concept of speed and its relationship to the concepts of rate. In G. Harel & J. Confrey (Eds.), *The development of multiplicative reasoning in the learning of mathematics* (pp. 181–234). Albany, NY: State University of New York Press.

Thompson, P., & Saldanha, L. (2000). *To understand post-counting numbers and operations.* Unpublished white paper prepared for the National Council of Teachers of Mathematics.

Ursini, S. (1994). Ambientes Logo como apoyo para trabajar las nociones de variación y correspondencia [Logo environments as support to work on notions of variation and correspondence]. In *Memoria del primer simposio sobre metodología de la enseñanza de las matemáticas* (pp. 124–128). Mexico City, México: Instituto Tecnológico Autónomo de México.

Ursini, S. (1997). El lenguaje Logo, los niños y las variables [Logo language, children and variables]. *Educación Matemática, 9*(2), 30–42.

Ursini, S. (2001). General methods: A way of entering the world of algebra. In R. Sutherland, T. Rojano, A. Bell, & R. Lins (Eds.), *Perspectives on school algebra* (pp. 209–230). Dordrecht, The Netherlands: Kluwer.

Usiskin, Z. (1988). Conceptions of school algebra and uses of variables. In A. Coxford & A. Shulte (Eds.), *The ideas of algebra, K–12. 1988 Yearbook* (pp. 8–19). Reston, VA: The National Council of Teachers of Mathematics.

Vergnaud, G. (1983). Multiplicative structures. In R. Lesh & M. Landau (Eds.), *Acquisition of mathematics: Concepts and process* (pp. 189–199). New York: Academic Press.

Vergnaud, G. (1985). Understanding mathematics at the secondary-school level. In A. Bell, B. Low, & J. Kilpatrick (Eds.), *Theory, research & practice in mathematical education* (pp. 27–45). Nottingham, UK: Shell Center for Mathematical Education.

Vergnaud, G. (1988). Long terme et court terme dans l'apprentissage de l'algèbre [Long term and short term in learning algebra]. In C. Laborde (Ed.), *Actes du premier colloque franco-allemand de didactique des mathematiques et de l'informatique* (pp. 189–199). Paris: La Pensée Sauvage.

Vergnaud, G. (1994). Multiplicative conceptual field: What and why? In G. Harel & J. Confrey (Eds.), *The development of multiplicative reasoning in the learning of mathematics* (pp. 41–60). Albany, NY: State University of New York Press.

Vergnaud, G., Cortes, A., & Favre-Artigue, P. (1988). Introduction de l'algèbre auprès des débutants faibles: Problèmes épistemologiques et didactiques. In G. Vergnaud, G. Brousseau, & M. Hulin (Eds.), *Didactique et acquisitions des connaissances scientifiques: Actes du Colloque de Sèvres* (pp. 259–280). Sèvres, France: La Pensée Sauvage.

Verschaffel, L., Greer, B., & De Corte, E. (2002). Everyday knowledge and mathematical modeling of school word problems. In K. Gravemeijer, R. Lehrer, B. Oers, & L. Verschaffel (Eds.), *Symbolizing, modeling and tool use in mathematics education* (pp. 249–268). The Netherlands: Kluwer.

Vygotsky, L. S. (1978). *Mind in society*. Cambridge, MA: Harvard University Press.

Wagner, S. (1981). Conservation of equation and function under transformations of variable. *Journal for Research in Mathematics Education, 12*, 107–118.

Warren, E. (2001). Algebraic understanding: The importance of learning in the early years. In H. Chick, K. Stacey, J. Vincent, & J. Vincent (Eds.), *The future of the teaching and learning of algebra: Proceedings of the 12th ICMI Study Conference* (Vol. 2, pp. 633–640). Melbourne, Australia: The University of Melbourne.

Yerushalmy, M., & Schwartz, J. (1993). Seizing the opportunity to make algebra mathematically and pedagogically interesting. In T. Romberg, E. Fennema, & T. Carpenter (Eds.), *Integrating research on the graphical representation of functions* (pp. 41–68). Hillsdale, NJ: Lawrence Erlbaum Associates.

Author Index

139

Subject Index

CD-ROM ACCOMPANIES BOOK
SHELVED AT CIRCULATION DESK

DATE DUE
